ATLAS VALE

The GenZ Manifesto

Shaping the Future, Redefining Reality

Contents

Introduction

We Are Change – The Era of Gen Z

Hey, change-maker.

Yeah, *you*. The one scrolling endlessly, laughing at memes, debating politics, fighting for climate justice, and dreaming about creating a world that looks *different*.

You've probably heard people say, *"Gen Z is just a bunch of lazy, entitled kids."* But here's the truth: that narrative couldn't be more wrong.

You aren't lazy. You're *conscious*, *connected*, and *committed.*

You've grown up in a world that taught you resilience—not just through textbooks, but through TikToks, climate catastrophes, and global protests. You've learned that change doesn't wait— it demands action, immediacy, and relentless commitment.

Our generation is reshaping reality. Climate change? Mental health crises? Social inequalities? These aren't just news headlines anymore—they're the realities we navigate every day.

But here's the secret sauce: You're not just living in these realities—you're transforming them.

We've got the tools: digital platforms, global networks, and a voice that resonates *worldwide*. We have purpose-driven hearts, a deep connection to mental well-being, and a commitment to justice that transcends borders. We don't just talk about change—we drive it.

This book isn't just about activism, productivity, or personal growth—it's a manifesto. A call to arms. A roadmap for turning your passion, your doubts, and your dreams into *real-world action*.

Together, let's stop waiting for permission. Let's stop being sidelined by challenges. This is about purpose. About power. About persistence. It's about knowing that **every single thing you do creates a ripple effect** that can change lives, cities, and even nations.

Welcome to **your movement**. Welcome to **your legacy**.

Let's stop talking about change. Let's start making it.

INTRODUCTION

1

The Power of Our Generation

Who Are We, Really?

Quick Stats About Gen Z

Let's get real: you're not just another demographic. You're a powerful force shaping *every* sector of life, from tech to politics, from education to activism.

Here's what defines **Gen Z** (born roughly between 1997 and 2012):

- **Digital Natives:**
- 98% of Gen Z own a smartphone (source: Pew Research Center).
- The average Gen Z individual spends **up to 4 hours a day on social media** platforms like TikTok, Instagram, and Snapchat.

- More than 60% of Gen Z prefer to communicate *digitally* rather than face-to-face.

- **Diverse Generation:**
- Gen Z is the **most racially and ethnically diverse generation** in history. In the U.S., 48% of Gen Z is made up of ethnic minorities, including Black, Hispanic, and Asian communities (source: Pew Research Center).
- This diversity shapes a generation committed to inclusivity and representation in media, workplaces, and politics.

- **Education & Ambition:**
- Approximately **59% of Gen Z students want to start their own business**, showcasing an entrepreneurial spirit from a young age (source: Forbes).
- A significant portion of Gen Z prioritizes **self-education**, with millions turning to platforms like YouTube, Coursera, and Khan Academy to learn new skills.

- **Financial Awareness:**
- Around **73% of Gen Z prefer saving money over spending**, showing a cautious and investment-oriented mindset (Nielsen Insights).
- Gen Z values *financial stability*, often seeking to invest in experiences, education, and ethical products.

What Sets Us Apart

We aren't just adapting to the world as it is—we're fundamentally reshaping it. Gen Z stands out from every generation that came before, not only because of how we grew up but because of what we stand for. Here's what truly sets us apart:

Digital Natives at the Core

Unlike any other generation, we've been immersed in technology from the start. For us, the internet isn't a tool—it's a language we've spoken fluently since childhood. Platforms like Instagram, TikTok, and YouTube didn't just entertain us; they educated us, connected us, and gave us the power to amplify our voices.

We don't passively consume media. Instead, we curate, create, and challenge it. This ability to shape the digital landscape has redefined the boundaries of communication and activism. In fact, over **60% of Gen Z** believe that social media allows them to engage in causes they care about (source: Pew Research).

We don't just browse the web; we build movements. Climate strikes, social justice campaigns, and mental health advocacy aren't just initiatives—they're hashtags, viral challenges, and global conversations. Our digital fluency is the reason why ideas once confined to local spaces now ignite global change.

Resilient in the Face of Crisis

The world we've grown up in hasn't been gentle, but it's taught us to adapt, endure, and persist. Economic turbulence, school violence, the climate crisis, and a pandemic that halted life as we knew it—these weren't just headlines for us. They were our formative years.

But instead of breaking under the weight of these challenges, we've built a resilience that defines us. Studies show that **Gen Z is more likely than older generations to see failure as a stepping stone** and prioritize mental health as a foundation for success (source: McKinsey & Company).

Our resilience isn't just reactive—it's proactive. We're the ones who demand change, push for reform, and challenge the status quo, not out of luxury but necessity. To us, survival isn't about staying afloat; it's about redefining the systems that aren't working.

Socially Conscious & Purpose-Driven

Gen Z is often called the "activist generation," and with good reason. We are deeply invested in issues like climate change, mental health, gender equality, and racial justice. But our passion goes beyond awareness—it translates into tangible action.

Over **70% of Gen Z consumers** are more likely to buy from companies that reflect their values (source: First Insight). Our generation demands accountability from businesses, governments, and institutions. This isn't just a trend; it's a shift in priorities.

Our purpose is grounded in inclusion. From calling out cultural appropriation to uplifting underrepresented voices, we believe that progress is only real if it's shared. Diversity isn't just a buzzword for us; it's a requirement.

We believe in **local action with global impact**. Whether it's championing sustainability through thrift shopping, support- ing fair-trade brands, or starting petitions for meaningful change, our efforts ripple outward.

Gen Z isn't just a demographic or a marketing label. We are a collective force of innovation, resilience, and action. We've inherited challenges, yes, but we've also built tools to address them—tools like technology, collaboration, and unwavering purpose.

The question isn't whether Gen Z will change the world. The question is: **How big will the impact be, and how quickly will it come?** Because if there's one thing we know, it's this: We don't just wait for change—we are the change.

Our World, Our Challenges

We live in an era defined by monumental challenges, but these same challenges bring unprecedented opportunities to reshape our future. The obstacles we face aren't just tests; they're invitations to innovate, collaborate, and act decisively.

Let's dive deeper into the pressing issues defining our generation and explore how we can rise to meet them head-on.

Climate Crisis: The Call for Urgency

The climate emergency is no longer a distant possibility—it's a lived reality. Floods, wildfires, and unpredictable weather patterns dominate headlines. This is our generation's defining challenge, demanding immediate and lasting action.

- **Escalating Impacts**: According to the IPCC, global temperatures have already risen by 1.1°C, and the consequences are severe. From rising sea levels to prolonged droughts, millions face displacement, food shortages, and poverty. Climate-induced events are responsible for a **20% decline in global crop yields** (FAO), further threatening global stability.
- **Our Role**: Gen Z isn't standing by. Surveys from the World Economic Forum show that **64% of us view climate change as the most pressing issue of our time**, with many taking action by advocating for sustainable policies, supporting renewable energy initiatives, and making conscious lifestyle choices like reducing waste and choosing eco-friendly products.

We have the tools to combat the crisis—technological advancements, grassroots movements, and the power of global connection. What's needed now is unyielding commitment and creative solutions.

Mental Health: The Silent Epidemic

In a hyper-connected world, the pressures on mental health are immense. For Gen Z, balancing productivity, social media, and personal expectations creates an environment ripe for stress and burnout.

- **The Statistics Are Stark**: Reports from the National Institute of Mental Health reveal that **1 in 4 Gen Z individuals struggles with anxiety, depression, or related issues.** Social media plays a dual role: it fosters connection but also fuels comparison and inadequacy.
- **Cultural Shifts**: Despite the challenges, Gen Z is breaking the stigma surrounding mental health. More of us seek therapy and talk openly about struggles than any prior generation. We recognize that emotional well-being isn't optional; it's foundational to personal and collective progress.

By normalizing conversations, demanding systemic support, and showing empathy, we're shaping a world where mental health is prioritized. Our goal isn't just surviving the pressures—it's thriving in spite of them.

Economic Instability: Redefining Success

For Gen Z, economic stability often feels out of reach. Student debt, high housing costs, and job market uncertainty paint a bleak picture. Yet, we are finding new ways to navigate this landscape.

- **Economic Realities**: In the U.S. alone, student debt totals over **$1.5 trillion**, with Gen Z shouldering much of this burden. Rising inflation and stagnant wages mean that many work multiple jobs to stay afloat.

- **Reshaping the Narrative**: Despite these hurdles, Gen Z is redefining success. A Nielsen report highlights that **73% of us prefer saving over spending**, and entrepreneurship is on the rise. From freelancing to investing in cryptocurrency, we're exploring unconventional paths to financial independence.

This generation is challenging outdated norms. We're blending financial sustainability with personal fulfillment, proving that wealth isn't just measured in dollars but in opportunities and balance.

Social Justice Movements: The Fight for Equality

Social justice is woven into the fabric of Gen Z's identity. From climate strikes to gender equality protests, we've shown time and again that activism isn't an extracurricular activity—it's a core part of who we are.

- **Harnessing Technology for Change**: Gen Z uses social media not just for awareness but as a platform for action. Tools like Instagram and TikTok have amplified movements like **Black Lives Matter** and global climate protests.
- **Demanding Accountability**: A survey by First Insight reveals that **80% of Gen Z expects brands to take a stand on social issues.** This demand for transparency extends to governments and institutions, pushing them toward inclusivity and fairness.

We're dismantling outdated structures and advocating for justice in all forms—racial equality, gender identity, and disability rights. Change isn't optional; it's a responsibility we embrace wholeheartedly.

Each of these challenges offers a moment to pause, reflect, and act. Gen Z isn't defined by the problems we face but by the solutions we create. With our innovation, resilience, and collective strength, we have the power to turn adversity into progress.

This is our world, our moment. The question isn't whether we'll make a difference—it's how far-reaching that difference will be. Will you join the movement?

Why Now is Our Moment

This is our time—a pivotal chapter in human history where the ability to change the world is in our hands, and the need for that change has never been more urgent. Standing at the intersection of innovation, history, and global challenges, we possess the tools, the perspective, and the resilience to drive profound transformation.

Let's explore the reasons this moment belongs to us and how we can maximize its potential.

Historical Perspective: Lessons from Youth-Led Movements

The power of youth is not a new phenomenon. Across decades, young people have spearheaded revolutions, demanded justice, and shaped cultural paradigms. These examples from history highlight our capacity to turn conviction into progress:

- **The Civil Rights Movement (1960s, U.S.):** Young activists in groups like the Student Nonviolent Coordinating Committee (SNCC) stood at the vanguard of the struggle against segregation. Their sit-ins, Freedom Rides, and marches didn't just change laws—they reshaped the moral fabric of a nation. Without their persistence, landmark legislation like the Civil Rights Act of 1964 might not exist today.
- **The Anti-Vietnam War Movement (1960s-1970s):** College campuses became the epicenter of resistance against the Vietnam War. Young people organized teach-ins, protests, and nationwide demonstrations that challenged government policies and ultimately influenced public opinion and policy.
- **The Arab Spring (2010s):** In nations like Tunisia and Egypt, youth harnessed social media to organize protests, share information, and demand accountability from oppressive regimes. Their bravery brought significant political shifts and inspired a global wave of movements for justice.

These stories prove a vital point: history turns on the hinge of youth action. And now, equipped with unparalleled tools and insight, we can amplify that legacy.

Why We Are Uniquely Positioned to Drive Change

While previous generations faced their own monumental challenges, we are uniquely equipped to address the crises of today with the tools and traits that define us.

Unprecedented Technological Tools

We are the first generation to come of age in a hyper-connected, tech-driven world. For us, technology is not a luxury—it's an extension of our voice and power.

- **Digital Advocacy:** Platforms like Instagram, TikTok, and Twitter have transformed activism. From climate strikes organized in hours to fundraisers reaching millions globally, technology lets us mobilize at unprecedented speed.
- **Shaping Public Opinion:** A 2022 Pew Research study found that **nearly 70% of Gen Z uses social media as their primary source of news.** This positions us as both consumers and creators of narratives, shaping discourse on issues from environmental policy to social justice.

With the click of a button, we can reach audiences that civil rights leaders of the past could only dream of.

A Truly Global Perspective

Unlike previous generations, we have grown up with access to a world where borders blur, and cultures intersect.

- **Awareness of Global Challenges:** From the climate crisis in the Arctic to social unrest in the Global South, we're acutely aware of how interconnected these issues are. A Deloitte survey reveals that **more than 75% of Gen Z believes tackling climate change should be a top priority.**
- **Collaboration Across Borders:** Social media, online forums,

and global campaigns have allowed us to forge alliances with peers around the world, sharing strategies and solutions. Movements like Fridays for Future demonstrate how localized action can evolve into global momentum.

Resilience in the Face of Adversity

We've been tested by crises—economic recessions, climate catastrophes, and a global pandemic. These experiences have shaped us into a generation of problem-solvers.

- **Adapting to Economic Uncertainty:** Saddled with student debt and soaring living costs, we've embraced entrepreneurship and nontraditional career paths. Freelancing, gig work, and digital ventures are increasingly common among us, reflecting our ability to innovate under pressure.
- **Mental Health Advocacy:** We are rewriting the narrative on mental health. Where silence once reigned, we now prioritize openness and support. A McKinsey report shows that **more than 50% of Gen Z actively seeks mental health resources,** challenging stigmas and pushing institutions to improve access.

The Challenges We Face

This generation doesn't lack obstacles. However, the magnitude of our challenges only underscores the urgency of action.

- **The Climate Crisis:** Rising sea levels, intensifying wildfires, and unpredictable weather patterns demand immediate intervention. According to the UN, the next decade is critical for limiting global warming to 1.5°C—a target that requires systemic change and individual commitment.

- **Social Inequities:** Issues like racial injustice, gender inequality, and systemic poverty remain pervasive. Yet, young people are demanding accountability, advocating for representation, and building movements to dismantle oppressive structures.

These are not insurmountable problems. They are calls to action.

Turning Potential into Progress

What distinguishes this moment is not just our ability to act but our determination to do so in ways that are inclusive, innovative, and impactful.

- **Building Coalitions:** Whether through local community organizing or global partnerships, collaboration remains key. The success of initiatives like #MeToo and Black Lives Matter proves that collective action is a force to be reckoned with.
- **Investing in Innovation:** From renewable energy startups to AI-powered social enterprises, young people are creating solutions that didn't exist a decade ago. Crowdfunding and micro-investing platforms enable us to scale our ideas rapidly.

Our ability to shape the future lies in our hands. Each of us has a role to play—whether as activists, entrepreneurs, or storytellers. The question isn't whether we will rise to the occasion but how far-reaching our impact will be.

The Time Is Now

We are the architects of tomorrow. The tools we wield, the communities we build, and the values we uphold will define not just our generation but the generations that follow.

This is our moment to rewrite the rules, dismantle barriers, and leave a legacy of progress. Let's take the lessons of history, combine them with our unique strengths, and drive the change the world so desperately needs.

Because if not us, then who? And if not now, then when?

Digital Tools as Amplifiers of Action

Digital tools have reshaped how we engage with the world. They're not just instruments of connection or platforms for expression—they've become catalysts for transformation, empowering individuals and communities to enact change at scales unimaginable a generation ago.

Social Media: A Mobilization Engine

Platforms like Instagram, TikTok, YouTube, and Twitter have evolved from social hubs into global arenas for activism. They amplify marginalized voices, highlight injustices, and mobilize movements almost instantaneously.

- **Examples of Impact:**The **Black Lives Matter** movement gained extraordinary momentum through social media. In the wake of George Floyd's murder, millions worldwide participated in protests organized via platforms like Instagram and Twitter. Hashtags like #BlackLivesMatter have been used over 100 million times, influencing policy discussions and corporate accountability.
- **Climate strikes**, championed by figures like Greta Thunberg, owe much of their success to digital advocacy. Twitter threads, viral TikTok videos, and Instagram reels galvanized millions to march for the planet.

With these tools, awareness spreads rapidly, pushing issues to the forefront of public discourse.

Crowdsourcing Ideas and Resources

Digital tools democratize the ability to support and scale meaningful initiatives. Crowdfunding platforms like **GoFundMe**, **Kickstarter**, and **Patreon** have redefined resource mobilization.

- **Breaking Barriers:**When traditional funding sources fall short, grassroots initiatives thrive. For example, during the COVID-19 pandemic, crowdfunding campaigns provided critical relief for small businesses and frontline workers.
- Artists, activists, and innovators bypass gatekeepers by connecting directly with supporters who share their vision. Patreon, for instance, allows creators to sustain their work through direct contributions from fans worldwide.

These platforms turn collective power into tangible action, proving that small contributions can create massive impact.

Global Activism Networks

The internet has erased geographic barriers, enabling communities to form around shared goals and causes. Platforms like **Reddit**, **Discord**, and **Slack** are essential tools for coordination and strategy.

- **Real-Time Collaboration:**Activists use **Discord servers** to plan rallies, exchange strategies, and provide emotional support.
- Subreddits like **r/ClimateActionPlan** unite environmental advocates, creating a space to brainstorm policies, share research, and encourage individual contributions.
- During the Hong Kong protests, encrypted messaging apps like Signal and Telegram ensured secure communication and helped protesters stay ahead of government crackdowns.

These tools connect people across continents, proving that no idea is too small and no location too remote.

AI and Machine Learning: Driving Innovation

Artificial intelligence is transforming activism and problem-solving. From analyzing massive datasets to crafting targeted interventions, AI empowers changemakers to tackle complex issues with precision.

- **Applications in Action:Climate Action:** AI models analyze weather patterns, predict climate risks, and recommend mitigation strategies. Tools like Google's AI-driven **Global Fishing Watch** use satellite data to combat illegal fishing.
- **Education:** Personalized learning platforms powered by AI—like Khan Academy's AI tutors—address gaps in education by tailoring content to individual needs.
- **Mental Health:** AI chatbots, such as Woebot, provide accessible mental health support, addressing stigma and resource scarcity in underserved areas.

By integrating these tools, we create smarter, more efficient solutions to the world's toughest challenges.

Responsibility Meets Opportunity

As digital natives, we are uniquely positioned to wield these tools responsibly and effectively. Our generation must recognize the power at our fingertips and use it to solve problems that were once considered insurmountable.

- **What We Can Do:Collaborate:** Build coalitions across platforms to strengthen campaigns.
- **Innovate:** Use emerging technologies creatively to solve social, economic, and environmental issues.
- **Educate:** Share knowledge to empower others to take action.

The world is looking for leaders who not only understand the challenges but are ready to rise to them. And that's where we step in—not as passive observers, but as active creators of a more inclusive, just, and sustainable future.

The Time to Act Is Now

Digital tools have leveled the playing field. They allow us to amplify voices, spark conversations, and create solutions. This isn't just an age of technology; it's an era of opportunity.

Let's harness these tools to challenge the status quo, empower communities, and drive meaningful change. The world isn't just waiting for us—it's depending on us.

Together, we can transform potential into progress and ensure a brighter tomorrow.

2

Clarity of Purpose – Define Your Why

Identifying Your Passions and Purpose

inding your purpose isn't about waiting for a sudden, life-changing revelation where everything just *clicks*. It's not a magical moment that comes out of nowhere. Instead, purpose is something that emerges through **active exploration, intentional questioning**, and **the deliberate act of creating meaning in your life**. It's about seeking opportunities, experimenting with possibilities, and learning through every experience—success or failure.

Passion and purpose aren't just about what makes you *happy* in the moment; they are the engines that drive **long-term fulfillment, resilience**, and **real-world impact**.

A passionate commitment to something that aligns with your

core values gives life a deeper meaning. It equips you with resilience during difficult times because when your work and life align with your purpose, setbacks become lessons rather than defeats.

When you pursue something that resonates with your heart and also addresses the challenges or needs of the world around you, the path ahead becomes less murky. You start to see opportunities rather than obstacles, and challenges become motivations rather than roadblocks. This intersection—where **your personal passion meets the greater needs of society or the environment**—is where purpose truly thrives.

What Purpose Really Means

Purpose isn't just for those who change history or make headlines. It's not always about global fame, monumental achievements, or massive social impact. At its core, purpose is the **reason behind your actions, your choices, and your path**. It's about what drives you, fuels your day, and gives your efforts a sense of direction and fulfillment. Purpose is about channeling your energy into something that feels **authentic, meaningful,** and **connected to who you are**.

Purpose Doesn't Always Have to Look Big—But It Should Feel Big to You

For some, purpose is about contributing meaningfully to their local community. It might mean **volunteering at a local shel-**

ter, mentoring a student, cleaning up a park, or **organizing community events**.

These actions are not about recognition; they're about **connection, responsibility**, and **impact at a personal level**. You realize purpose through service, collaboration, and commitment—through knowing that your contribution strengthens bonds and builds trust among people around you.

For others, purpose comes through **personal growth or creative endeavors**. It might be about writing a song, painting a mural, coding an app, or designing a new product. Here, purpose is about **expressing yourself authentically and contributing your unique voice**. It's about self-discovery, skill development, and resilience. Creative expression often becomes a journey of **self-realization and emotional balance**, teaching discipline and focus along the way.

Why Purpose Is Crucial

Living without purpose often leads to feelings of **stagnation, apathy**, and **disconnection**. When you don't have a guiding principle or "why," it becomes harder to take initiative, stay motivated, and maintain a sense of direction. Time may feel wasted, actions become mechanical, and goals lose their meaning.

On the flip side, having a clear sense of purpose transforms even the smallest tasks into meaningful steps toward something greater. Purpose infuses your actions with **clarity, intention**, and **direction**.

The Tangible Benefits of Identifying Your Purpose

1. **Clarity**

When you have a clear purpose, decision-making becomes more straightforward. Instead of being paralyzed by endless choices, you have a guiding principle that helps you prioritize what matters most. You ask yourself, *"Does this align with what I stand for and want to achieve?"* This clarity minimizes uncertainty and maximizes focus. Research by psychologists like **Dr. Viktor Frankl**, author of *Man's Search for Meaning*, emphasizes that having a personal purpose can guide individuals in making better life choices.

2. **Resilience**

Purpose acts as your anchor during challenges. Knowing your "why" gives you the strength to persist through setbacks and obstacles. It reminds you that challenges are not just roadblocks but **opportunities for growth and learning**. Studies published in journals like **The Journal of Clinical Psychiatry** show that individuals with a strong sense of purpose experience **greater resilience**, bounce back from adversity faster, and possess a more optimistic outlook on life. When purpose is clear, setbacks don't feel like failures; they become **lessons in progress and self-improvement**.

3. **Fulfillment**

Purpose transforms effort into meaningful work. When you work on something that you care about deeply, your daily actions don't just become tasks—they become opportunities for fulfillment. Whether it's through creative expression, helping others, or professional endeavors, having purpose-driven goals ensures that your time and energy contribute to something **worthwhile and satisfying**. Research from **Harvard Health Publishing** indicates that individuals who have a purpose-driven life report higher levels of **job satisfaction, mental health**, and **overall happiness**.

Purpose and Society

Having a sense of purpose doesn't just benefit the individual—it also strengthens society. Purpose-driven individuals are more likely to **engage in community activities, support social causes**, and drive initiatives that uplift others.

Studies in **The American Journal of Preventive Medicine** show that purpose-oriented people tend to contribute positively to their communities, volunteering more often and helping others, which strengthens social bonds and community resilience.

How to Identify Your Passions and Purpose

Finding your purpose isn't a one-time revelation; it's a continuous process of **introspection, exploration**, and **action**. It takes time and self-awareness, but you can take practical steps to guide yourself toward clarity. Here are some actionable strategies to help you uncover your purpose step by step.

1. Reflect on Your Interests and Curiosity

Start by asking yourself **simple but profound questions**:

- What excites me?
- What activities make me lose track of time?
- Which subjects do I naturally gravitate toward without being asked?

Passion often springs from **curiosity and genuine enthusiasm**, not obligation. It could be working with your hands, solving technical challenges, or diving deep into social discussions.

- If you love **creating things**, perhaps your purpose lies in **design, innovation**, or **engineering**.
- If you feel energized by **social interactions**, maybe you find purpose in **community work, teaching**, or **team leadership**.

Reflect on moments when you felt **fully immersed** and connected. These experiences often hint at what you care about deeply.

2. Examine Your Core Values

Your core values act as **signposts**, guiding your purpose and aligning your actions with what truly matters to you. Common values include **honesty, compassion, creativity, justice**, and **curiosity**. Knowing these can help you make choices that align with your inner compass.

- **Write Down Your Top Values:** Make a list of 5-10 values that resonate strongly with you.
- Ask yourself, **"How do these values show up in my daily**

life?"

- Reflect on moments where you felt truly **fulfilled, connected**, or **empowered**. What core values were present in those experiences?

For instance, if **justice** is a core value, your purpose might drive you to **advocate for marginalized communities** or **support human rights initiatives**.

3. Pay Attention to What Bothers You

Sometimes, your purpose reveals itself through **frustrations, injustices**, and **social issues** that stir a sense of responsibility within you. If you notice something that bothers you deeply, consider that it might be a sign of where your energy and purpose should go.

- Are you **disturbed by environmental degradation**? Maybe sustainability and eco-activism should be part of your journey.
- Do issues of **mental health, inequality**, or **discrimination** make you feel compelled to act? Think about how you could contribute—through awareness campaigns, social initiatives, or community support.

This approach aligns with research suggesting that **social responsibility and activism** often drive individuals to find deeper purpose and long-term commitment (**Psychological Bulletin**, 2008).

4. Identify Your Strengths and Talents

Your purpose should leverage what you're **naturally good at,** making your goals more achievable and sustainable. Knowing your strengths connects your **capabilities** with meaningful endeavors.

- Ask yourself:
- What tasks do I find easy, while others struggle?
- Which activities make me feel confident and energized?
- How have friends or mentors described my strengths?

Use tools like the **StrengthsFinder Assessment**, or simply seek **honest feedback** from people who know you well. Whether it's **problem-solving, communication**, or **artistic expression**, aligning your skills with a meaningful purpose creates a sense of flow and satisfaction.

For example, someone good at **data analysis** might find purpose in **creating tech solutions for social impact**, while someone strong in **writing** might focus on **advocacy campaigns** or **content creation for education**.

5. Experiment, Take Risks, and Learn

Purpose is not always a destination—it's often discovered through **action, experimentation**, and **experience**. Don't wait for perfect clarity. Instead, start trying new things and exploring different opportunities.

- Volunteer at a local community center
- Join grassroots movements or nonprofit initiatives
- Start a personal project, even if it's small
- Collaborate with peers on initiatives that align with social

or professional goals

Each experiment, whether it succeeds or fails, offers valuable insights. It helps you learn what you enjoy, where your strengths lie, and what kind of impact you want to make. In the words of **Thomas Edison**, *"I have not failed. I've just found 10,000 ways that won't work."*

Each experience is a step closer to discovering what your purpose truly is.

Your Journey Toward Purpose

You don't need to have it all figured out today. Purpose is a process, not a destination. As you explore your passions, reflect on your values, and experiment with new experiences, your purpose will reveal itself in layers.

Start small. Ask yourself:

- What do I care about deeply?
- How can I contribute to something bigger than myself?
- What legacy do I want to leave behind?

Remember, purpose doesn't have to be grand to be meaningful—it just has to be yours.

Discovering Your Passions

Finding your passions is less about chasing what's trendy and more about recognizing what feels natural, exciting, and fulfilling. It's about tuning into the activities and moments where you lose track of time and feel genuinely alive.

Ask Yourself the Right Questions

- What do I do for fun, even when no one asks or pays me?
- When do I feel most energized and creative?
- What subjects or activities have always intrigued me?

Passion often emerges when curiosity meets enjoyment. For example:

- If you love building or fixing things, your passion could lie in engineering, design, or crafting.
- If storytelling excites you, it could be writing, filmmaking, or speaking.

Passions don't always start as clear "eureka" moments. They unfold as you experiment with different activities and notice what resonates deeply.

Find Your Sweet Spot

True passion often sits at the intersection of:

1. **What You Love:** Activities that light you up.
2. **What You're Good At:** Skills and talents that come naturally or that you're willing to work hard to develop.
3. **What the World Needs:** Ways you can contribute to others or solve problems meaningfully.

This alignment transforms enthusiasm into purpose-driven passion. Think of chefs who blend a love for food with sustainability or educators who spark change by inspiring future generations.

Why Purpose Drives Change

Having purpose connects your passion to meaningful action. It shifts your focus from "What can I gain?" to "What can I contribute?"

The Power of Purpose

- **Inspires and Unites:** Purpose-driven individuals don't just pursue goals—they rally others toward shared visions.
- **Boosts Resilience:** A clear "why" helps you overcome failures and setbacks because the end goal is bigger than temporary struggles.
- **Fuels Productivity:** Studies reveal that people with purpose

are happier, healthier, and more engaged in their work 7 source8 source.

Purpose transforms small acts into meaningful contributions. Whether your focus is personal growth, career success, or social change, a purpose-centered mindset amplifies your impact.

Embracing Your Purpose Step by Step

Finding and living your purpose is a process, not an overnight discovery. Start small and build steadily.
   Practical Steps:

1. **Schedule Time for Reflection:**

- Revisit moments where you felt proud, fulfilled, or excited.
- Identify patterns in your interests and actions.

1. **Engage with Role Models:**

- Seek conversations with people who inspire you.
- Learn how they discovered and pursued their passions despite challenges.

1. **Take Notes and Reflect Often:**

- Keep a journal of your thoughts and realizations.
- Writing helps clarify your thoughts and track your growth.

1. **Experiment and Act:**

- Volunteer for causes that resonate with you.
- Try new hobbies, join groups, or start small projects.

Purpose isn't just a feeling—it's an action. By experimenting, learning, and growing, you'll naturally uncover what matters most.

Your Purpose in Practice

Purpose doesn't have to be groundbreaking. It's about doing what feels meaningful to you while making an impact on others, no matter how small.

Remember: You don't find your passions and purpose overnight—they reveal themselves in the doing. Take the first step today, and let the journey guide you.

Purpose is Your Superpower

Purpose isn't just a concept—it's a force that transforms how you live and what you achieve. It gives direction to your choices, fuels your persistence, and infuses every action with meaning. Think of it as a compass and a power source, rolled into one.

What Makes Purpose So Powerful?

1. **Clarity in Decision-Making**
2. When your purpose is clear, decisions become easier. You stop second-guessing yourself because you know what aligns with your values and goals. For instance, if your purpose revolves around sustainability, you naturally lean towards eco-friendly habits and initiatives without hesitation.
3. **Resilience in the Face of Setbacks**
4. Purpose gives you a reason to keep going, even when the road is rough. You see obstacles as stepping stones rather than dead ends. Nelson Mandela, who endured decades of imprisonment, stayed resilient because of his unwavering purpose: to end apartheid and bring justice to South Africa.
5. **Motivation for Impact**
6. Purpose ties your actions to something bigger than yourself. This connection creates intrinsic motivation. Whether it's building communities, driving social reform, or innovating in your field, purpose amplifies your drive and focus.

Purpose: A Catalyst for Connection

Purpose doesn't just empower you—it also draws others to your mission. Shared purpose fosters authentic connections, inspiring collaboration and collective action. Think of global movements like climate action, where individuals with shared goals come together to create massive change.

When you align with people who share your purpose, your potential for impact multiplies. Collaboration can turn a small idea into a movement, a project into a revolution.

The Tools to Amplify Your Purpose

We live in an era where purpose-driven actions can ripple globally. Tools like social media, crowdfunding platforms, and AI-powered solutions enable you to scale your efforts and reach people across continents.

- **Social Media:** Use platforms to spread awareness, rally support, and mobilize action for causes you care about.
- **Crowdfunding:** Tap into resources like GoFundMe to fund initiatives and bring visions to life.
- **Digital Collaboration:** Leverage tools like Slack or Discord to build networks and strategize with like-minded individuals.

With the right tools, your purpose doesn't stay confined to your personal sphere—it grows into a force for broader impact.

Purpose Fuels Innovation and Creativity

Purpose drives you to challenge norms, think outside the box, and explore uncharted territories. Some of the most ground-breaking innovations and art have emerged from individuals deeply connected to their purpose:

- **Steve Jobs:** Revolutionized technology with a purpose centered on creating intuitive, beautiful tools for people.
- **Frida Kahlo:** Poured her purpose into art that expressed identity, resilience, and activism.

Your purpose can serve as the lens through which creativity flows, producing work that is not only original but deeply impactful.

Your Purpose is the "Why" Behind the "What"

Purpose answers the big question: *Why do I do this?* It's the reason you dedicate your energy to something, the "why" that gives depth to your efforts.

When purpose drives your actions, you inspire those around you to look deeper, think bigger, and act with more intention. This ripple effect of purpose can lead to change at both personal and societal levels.

Finding your purpose is just the first step. Living it out requires ongoing commitment and action.

- **Start Small:** Identify one way to align your daily actions with your purpose.
- **Reflect Often:** Regularly evaluate whether your efforts resonate with your values.

- **Stay Flexible:** Purpose can evolve as you grow, and that's okay.

Your purpose isn't just your superpower—it's the spark that lights up the lives of those around you. It's what turns dreams into reality and creates change that lasts.

This is your time. Use your purpose to lead, inspire, and create.

Goal Setting for Impact

Setting goals isn't just about ticking boxes or meeting deadlines. It's about creating **real change**—in your life, in your community, and in the world. You need to set goals that fuel your purpose, that challenge you, and that ultimately drive you to take meaningful action.

Goals should be ambitious but achievable.

By setting intentional, purpose-driven goals, you're not just checking off tasks—you're creating ripples of change. Every small step builds momentum, and before you know it, those steps become strides toward a life of greater meaning and impact.

Start today. Define one goal that excites you, aligns with your purpose, and challenges you just enough. The journey starts now, and it's one worth taking.

They should push boundaries but still be within reach. This is where the SMART framework comes in.

What Are SMART Goals?

You've probably heard of SMART goals before. It's a well-established method for setting objectives that have clarity, focus, and purpose.

But let's break down each element in a way that connects with you as an activist, creative, and changemaker.

Specific: Don't just say, *"I want to make a difference."* That's too vague. Instead, ask yourself: What exactly do I want to change? Is it about reducing waste in your community, growing your coding skills, or organizing a local awareness campaign? The more specific you are, the clearer your path will be.

Measurable: Goals need to have a way to measure progress. Instead of *"I want to be successful"*, say, *"I want to grow my social media following by 5,000 in three months."* This gives you a tangible target and a benchmark to track your progress.

Achievable: Ambition is essential, but setting unattainable goals only leads to frustration. Ask yourself: Is this goal realistic given my resources, time, and current skills? Adjust it if needed. Purpose-driven change often starts small but builds momentum over time.

Relevant: A goal should matter deeply to your purpose. Does it align with what you care about and want to achieve in your life? If your goal doesn't connect to your passions or your vision, it's just another task rather than a meaningful step forward.

Time-Bound: Set a deadline. Without a timeline, there's no urgency. A clear timeframe gives you a commitment to work towards. Whether it's a week, a month, or a year, a deadline keeps you accountable and motivated.

Why SMART Goals Drive Impact

Having a purpose without a clear path forward can feel like spinning your wheels without traction. SMART goals provide that needed structure to channel your passion and vision into actionable steps that make a difference.

The Power of SMART Goals

SMART goals—specific, measurable, achievable, relevant, and time-bound—help you move from wishful thinking to purposeful action. Here's how:

- **Clarity**: They help you define exactly what success looks like.

- **Focus**: By narrowing your priorities, you avoid distractions and work efficiently.
- **Accountability**: Measurable criteria make it easier to track progress and identify areas for improvement.
- **Adaptability**: If challenges arise, the structured nature of SMART goals helps you pivot without losing momentum.

For example, consider the goal: *"I want to help the environment."* It's inspiring but vague. Transforming it into a SMART goal— *"Reduce single-use plastics in my household by 80% within six months through reusable alternatives"*—makes it actionable and achievable.

Purpose Meets Progress

When goals align with your purpose, every step forward creates ripple effects. Take a community initiative to reduce plastic use in schools. A SMART goal might be:

> "Reduce plastic consumption in the school cafeteria by 50% within three months by replacing disposable containers with reusable ones and promoting eco-friendly options."

Turning Setbacks Into Opportunities

SMART goals not only clarify what success looks like but also prepare you to handle challenges. When setbacks occur, you can analyze why progress stalled, refine your approach, and move forward with renewed focus.

For instance, if the cafeteria goal faces resistance due to costs, the team can pivot by seeking donations or grants for initial reusable container purchases. Challenges become part of the process, not insurmountable roadblocks.

When individuals or groups embrace SMART goals, the results are powerful. Goals provide a roadmap for turning dreams into reality. Whether it's creating change in your local community, advancing your career, or working on personal growth, the structure they offer ensures every effort counts.

So, what's your next step? Define a SMART goal today—something meaningful and actionable—and start taking purposeful strides toward the impact you want to create.

Challenges and How to Overcome Them

Even with SMART goals, things won't always go smoothly. Life is unpredictable, and progress is rarely a straight line. But challenges are opportunities to grow, refine your goals, and strengthen your commitment.

If you miss a deadline, don't see your impact as a failure. Instead, analyze why things didn't work out.

Was the goal too ambitious? Did you not have the resources you needed? Did circumstances change in a way you didn't anticipate?

Adjust your goals as needed. Purpose-driven people don't abandon goals at the first obstacle—they adapt.

Every setback is a chance to learn and improve your strategy. The key is **resilience** and **adaptability**—traits that are core strengths of your generation.

Turning Goals into Action

Having a goal means committing to action. You need a plan. Outline the steps required to achieve your goal and break it into manageable tasks. What can you do this week? This month? This year?

Start with a clear plan and adjust as you move forward. Whether it's learning a new skill, raising awareness, or organizing an event, each step should bring you closer to your end goal.

Share your plans with friends, ask for feedback, and collaborate with others. Collective effort amplifies impact.

Your network, your community, and your digital presence are

all tools you can use to drive change.

Making Your Impact Sustainable

True impact is not a quick win—it's a commitment. Set up systems and habits that sustain your progress.

Whether it means dedicating time weekly to your initiatives, creating long-term community partnerships, or refining your skills continuously, sustainability ensures your efforts don't fade away.

Sustainable goals mean thinking about scalability, long-term engagement, and continuous improvement.

It's about creating habits and actions that maintain relevance and commitment over time.

When your goals are sustainable, your impact lasts. And with lasting impact comes change—real, significant, and far-reaching change.

Collective Purpose: Strength in Numbers

Strength is amplified when people come together with a shared purpose. As a generation deeply connected by social media, global trends, and collective values, you have the power to harness this collective energy to drive real and meaningful change.

You don't just have to pursue your personal goals—you can align those goals with your community's ambitions and contribute to a global impact.

When personal purpose meets collective intention, real transformation happens. It's about moving from **individual ambition** to **collective impact**, where everyone's unique strengths contribute to something bigger than just personal success. This is how your generation can shape a more resilient, socially aware, and purposeful world.

The Power of Collective Purpose

Historically, change has often come from collective action. Think about youth-led movements like the civil rights movement, the anti-war protests of the 1960s, or the environmental initiatives you see today.

These movements weren't driven by single individuals—they were fueled by **teams, communities, and shared determination**. Similarly, your collective purpose as Gen Z can drive significant social, environmental, and economic change.

When you align your personal goals with the goals of your community and the wider world, you bring in different perspectives, skills, and experiences.

Diversity strengthens your impact. It creates a synergy where what one person does can lift others, where cooperation becomes more effective than competition, and where your collective efforts drive systemic change rather than short-lived wins.

Aligning Personal Goals with Community Purpose

Every community—local, digital, or global—has challenges and opportunities. Your personal goals should not exist in isolation. Instead, think about how your ambition connects to the needs and aspirations of those around you.

If you're passionate about **sustainable living**, your personal interest in eco-friendly practices could align with community projects to reduce plastic waste in local schools or host neighborhood sustainability fairs.

Your desire to promote **mental health awareness** could connect with schools or online communities where collective efforts create supportive networks and meaningful change.

Start by asking yourself questions:

- What issues matter most to me?
- How can my skills and passion contribute to a bigger picture?
- Which community initiatives or global movements align with what I want to achieve?

For example, if you love tech and coding, you could contribute to community projects that use technology to improve education access. If you care about mental health, you could start a peer support group where sharing stories and resources empowers everyone.

Embracing Diversity and Inclusion

Collective purpose thrives on **diversity and inclusion**. It means recognizing that different cultures, experiences, and perspectives bring strength to your collective goals.

Diversity isn't just a buzzword—it's a crucial asset in any meaningful movement.

When you align your personal goals with a community purpose, you bring together different voices, each contributing valuable insights. This diversity means better problem-solving, more creativity, and a deeper, more inclusive impact. For example, consider initiatives that address global climate change. A community project tackling environmental issues would benefit from the experience of engineers, artists, students, and indigenous communities.

Each group has unique knowledge and experiences that together create innovative and effective solutions.

You, as a member of Gen Z, have grown up witnessing global

challenges firsthand—climate change, social movements, economic shifts, and mental health crises. This experience gives you a unique perspective.

You understand the interconnectedness of issues better than any previous generation. You recognize that social justice, mental health, and environmental sustainability are not separate topics—they are deeply interconnected realities that require a collective approach.

When you align your personal ambitions with community goals and global purpose, you become part of a bigger picture of systemic change. Your digital fluency and commitment to social justice create networks of support, innovation, and action that drive change faster and deeper.

Collective purpose isn't just about **achieving goals**; it's about **empowering people, transforming systems, and shaping a future where change is continuous, inclusive, and impactful.**

Moving Forward Together

Start small but think big. Build collective efforts in your community, online spaces, and among your peers. Focus on creating projects that align your personal interests with the needs of others.

Use your voice, your skills, and your digital presence to inspire and create change.

Remember, a collective purpose means lifting others as you climb. It's about contributing to projects that make the world better—not just for yourself, but for your community, your nation, and the global landscape. Your purpose grows stronger as more people join the effort, bringing their talents, passion, and commitment to the mission.

As Gen Z, you aren't just consumers of change—you're **creators, collaborators, and change-makers**. Strength in numbers means that together, with purpose and commitment, you can drive movements that change the world.

3

Knowledge is Power

Critical Media Literacy

In an age where digital information flows faster than ever before, media literacy is no longer just a valuable skill—it's a crucial safeguard for personal empowerment, critical thinking, and social engagement. Every day, you engage with an overwhelming amount of content: news articles, social media updates, podcasts, videos, blogs, and influencer stories.

While this constant influx of information offers incredible opportunities for learning and connection, it also brings significant challenges.

The reality is that not everything you see and hear online, on TV, or even in traditional media, is accurate, unbiased, or trustworthy. In fact, misinformation, propaganda, and media bias are thriving in today's digital landscape, often spreading faster than the truth.

Why Media Literacy Is Essential

Media literacy is about more than just knowing how to use social media or spot a catchy headline—it's about actively engaging with the information you consume and developing the skills to analyze, evaluate, and interpret media critically.

As a member of Gen Z, media literacy equips you with the tools to make well-informed decisions and take responsibility for your role as an informed citizen. It allows you to engage in meaningful discussions, contribute to healthy debates, and even challenge narratives that may be harmful or misleading. In other words, media literacy is a foundation of self-empowerment and social responsibility.

You're not just a consumer of media—you're a participant in shaping public discourse, influencing communities, and driving change. This means you need the ability to see beyond surface-level narratives, question sources, and recognize when media is trying to sway opinions or promote a specific agenda.

Dissecting Misinformation

Misinformation isn't a new phenomenon, but the scale and speed at which it spreads today are amplified by social media algorithms and digital platforms. Social media has made it possible for a single piece of content—a tweet, a Facebook post, an Instagram reel—to reach millions of people within minutes. While the speed of sharing can be empowering—raising awareness, driving solidarity, and creating change—it also creates a double-edged sword where false information can spread just as quickly as verified facts.

Misinformation comes in multiple forms:

1. **Fake News**: Often created intentionally to deceive or manipulate, fake news aims to spread lies quickly for financial or political gains.
2. **Clickbait Headlines**: Headlines designed to attract attention rather than inform. Phrases like "You Won't Believe This!" or "Secret Revealed" are designed to provoke curiosity rather than present truth.
3. **Propaganda**: Content that's intentionally created to push a political, social, or commercial agenda. It often includes persuasive language and visuals that appeal to emotions rather than logic.
4. **Biased Articles and News Outlets**: Sometimes, media outlets present stories with a clear bias, shaping public opinion by omitting crucial details or presenting information in a skewed way.
5. **Manipulated Visuals**: Photos and videos can be altered through editing software to misrepresent reality. Filters, cropping, and Photoshop are often tools for manipulation rather than honest storytelling.

Sometimes, misinformation is spread unintentionally due to

poor journalism, lack of research, or reliance on secondhand sources. In such cases, it may not be a deliberate attempt to mislead but still results in the distortion of facts and reality.

How to Identify Misinformation

Identifying misinformation requires a sharp eye and critical thinking skills. Here are some key strategies to help you spot false content:

Look for Sensational Language

- Media that uses **sensationalist language** often contains exaggerated claims meant to grab attention rather than present facts. Words like **"unbelievable," "shocking," "secret exposed," "exclusive reveal,"** and **"you won't believe"** are red flags that should prompt further scrutiny.

Evaluate the Source

- Ask yourself, **"Who is sharing this information, and what is their motive?"** Reliable news sources and credible journalists follow rigorous editorial standards. Websites without clear ownership or those that frequently mix opinion with news should be approached with caution.

Cross-Reference Information

- Verify facts by **checking multiple sources**. If an event or claim is important, reliable news outlets should have consistent coverage of it. Compare information across **respected media outlets, academic studies, and expert interviews**.

Analyze Visual Content Critically

- Photos and videos are often altered. Look for signs of editing—strange proportions, inconsistent lighting, or details that don't add up. Use **reverse image search tools** like Google Images to check if a photo has appeared elsewhere with a different context or timeline.

Check for Evidence and Attribution

- Credible stories include **verifiable evidence**, direct sources, and expert interviews. If claims are presented without clear evidence or credible citations, be skeptical.

Digital Literacy Tools

- Use fact-checking websites like **Snopes, FactCheck.org**, and **PolitiFact**, which analyze and validate claims circulating online. Many social platforms (Instagram, Twitter) also include **fact-check labels and warnings** that alert users to misinformation.

Media Literacy as a Social Responsibility

Understanding media literacy is about **individual awareness and collective responsibility**. In an interconnected world, misinformation can affect not only individuals but entire communities and nations. Misguided narratives can fuel misunderstanding, polarize opinions, and even spark social and political conflict.

When you critically engage with media, you are actively participating in creating a more informed, respectful, and cohesive society.

You have the responsibility to **share accurate information**, **challenge biased narratives**, and **support transparent, honest media sources**. Whether you're a social media user, a community member, or an activist, your commitment to media literacy can drive real social change by promoting transparency, truth, and accountability.

Being media literate means seeing beyond quick headlines and flashy images. It means asking questions, seeking answers, and standing up for what's true—not just in your personal experience but in your community and the broader society. It allows you to **amplify voices that deserve to be heard, dismantle harmful stereotypes, and stand against misinformation that threatens social cohesion and trust**.

Media literacy isn't just about protecting yourself—it's about empowering your community, fostering resilience, and standing up for informed discourse in every interaction, whether online or offline. It transforms you from a passive consumer of content into an active participant in shaping media narratives with responsibility, integrity, and purpose.

The Importance of Credible Sources

Knowing how to recognize credible sources is crucial. Not every website, social media post, or news outlet has the same commitment to truth, accuracy, or ethical journalism.

When you rely on trustworthy sources, you build your knowledge on a foundation of factual, objective information.

So, what makes a source credible?

1. **Transparency**: Reliable sources provide information about their ownership, editorial policies, and sources of funding. Are the authors identified? Is there an obvious bias? Transparency builds trust.
2. **Accountability**: Credible media outlets often have established editorial standards and fact-checking protocols. They issue corrections when mistakes occur, showing responsibility and honesty.
3. **Reputation**: Look at the history and reputation of media outlets. Established news organizations (e.g., BBC, NPR, Reuters) often follow rigorous journalistic standards.
4. **References and Sources**: A credible article or news piece cites sources and experts. If claims are backed by evidence and references to studies, interviews, or official reports,

you're more likely to have a reliable source.

In a media landscape inundated with content, discerning truth from misinformation requires a discerning approach. Prioritize news outlets that anchor their stories in **scientific research, authoritative studies, government reports**, and **expert interviews**, rather than hearsay, personal anecdotes, or anonymous claims.

By doing so, you contribute to a more informed society, uphold critical thinking, and foster media literacy that not only strengthens your perspective but also positively impacts your community and broader social discussions.

Spotting Bias and Objectivity

Media bias is a pervasive challenge in today's landscape. Every news outlet, social media influencer, and content creator has some degree of bias. These biases may stem from **political leanings, economic interests, social perspectives**, or even **cultural backgrounds**, and they shape how stories are told, facts are presented, and narratives are constructed.

Understanding and identifying bias allows you to consume media with a more discerning eye and make informed judgments about what you see and hear.

Media bias is not always overt or intentional. Often, it's embedded in the subtle choices a content creator makes, such as **language, tone, imagery, and the framing of facts**. These elements influence the narrative in ways that can subtly steer your perception, sometimes without you even realizing it.

The Influence of Ownership and Sponsorship

One of the first steps in spotting bias is considering **who owns the content and who is funding it**. Media outlets are often backed by corporations, political entities, or ideologically driven organizations, and these affiliations can have a signifi-cant impact on the content presented.

For instance, a news story from a media outlet with **clear political affiliations** might present facts in a way that supports a particular ideology or party agenda. Similarly, a company-sponsored article could emphasize certain viewpoints to pro-mote a product or service. This does not necessarily mean the information is false, but it should prompt you to scrutinize whether the source's interests align with their messaging.

Are they aiming to inform objectively, or is their goal to per-suade, sell, or manipulate public opinion?

Understanding sponsorships and ownership helps you gauge the intentions behind the content and assess whether any interests may distort the facts. It also encourages you to seek multiple perspectives from outlets with different affiliations, as this provides a more balanced view of the story.

Purpose and Motivation Behind the Message

Another crucial aspect of analyzing media bias is to ask yourself the **purpose behind the message**. What is the content creator's goal? Are they aiming to inform, persuade, or generate profit?

Content designed to **inform** typically focuses on accurate, well-sourced, and verifiable information. On the other hand, content created to **persuade** often includes persuasive language and emotional appeals. This kind of content might be seen in political campaigns, opinion pieces, or social media posts where the objective is to influence your beliefs or attitudes rather than present an unbiased truth.

Moreover, media created to **sell a product or service** usually contains language and imagery that focus on benefits and value rather than objective facts. Commercial content may rely on testimonials, influencer endorsements, and visually appealing presentations rather than factual accuracy or objective analysis.

By questioning the purpose of a message, you begin to separate **marketing hype, persuasive rhetoric**, and **political spin** from **factual reporting and objective analysis**. Ask yourself if the content prioritizes **truthfulness** and **transparency**, or if it serves an ulterior motive that might compromise the information presented.

Language, Framing, and Imagery

Content creators often use **specific language, framing techniques, and visuals** to subtly influence your interpretation of a story. Language can be loaded with emotional appeals, exaggerations, or persuasive words that elicit strong feelings rather than critical thought.

For example, news outlets sometimes use **sensational headlines** like "Shocking Discovery!" or "Unbelievable Revelation!" to grab attention. While these phrases might generate curiosity, they should prompt you to ask whether the claims are based on verifiable evidence or simply a way to attract views and clicks.

Visual elements are also powerful tools for shaping narratives. Images and videos are often carefully selected to **evoke emotions or highlight a particular perspective**. A photo of a protest, for instance, can be framed to show either the intensity of the event or the peaceful atmosphere, depending on the outlet's intention. Editing, cropping, and color adjustments can alter how viewers perceive reality. It's crucial to question whether these visuals accurately represent the context or if they're manipulated to support a specific point of view.

Recognizing Subtle Bias and Seeking Balance

Being media-savvy means going beyond the surface and questioning **what's not being said as much as what is being pre-**

sented. Often, stories omit certain viewpoints or facts to create a particular narrative. This omission can be intentional or accidental, but it still influences your understanding of the topic.

A balanced approach to media consumption involves actively seeking **multiple perspectives and viewpoints**. This might mean reading news articles from outlets with different political affiliations, listening to podcasts hosted by experts in various fields, or exploring content from international sources that offer a global perspective. Each source provides a different angle and helps form a more holistic understanding of the issue at hand.

Critical media literacy also means understanding **your own biases and perspectives**. Everyone brings their own experiences, beliefs, and background to how they interpret media. Recognizing your biases helps you engage more critically with the content you consume, allowing you to separate your opinions from the narratives presented by media outlets.

Digital Algorithms and Media Influence

Digital platforms like Instagram, TikTok, Twitter, and YouTube use algorithms designed to keep users engaged by showing content that appeals to their interests.

While these algorithms personalize your experience, they can also create **echo chambers** where you only see information that confirms your existing beliefs.

This personalization can limit your exposure to diverse viewpoints and information that challenges your perspective.

To combat this, actively seek out sources and accounts that represent different viewpoints, cultures, and ideologies. Follow news outlets and influencers with varying perspectives and engage in conversations that challenge your assumptions.

Algorithmic influence means that **critical thinking is your responsibility**. You must consciously seek multiple perspectives, diversify your sources, and question your biases rather than let digital tools do it for you.

Media Literacy as a Civic Responsibility

Being media literate is not just a personal skill—it's a social responsibility. You belong to a generation that is reshaping social norms, creating culture, and driving change.

Your ability to discern misinformation and recognize credible sources directly impacts your community, your social circle, and even global discourse.

Informed media consumers contribute to **healthy communities, responsible debates, and social change**. Whether you're discussing climate change, politics, social justice, or technology, your capacity to analyze and evaluate information strengthens your voice and enhances collective action.

Promote media literacy among your peers. Start initiatives in schools or online communities that focus on fact-checking challenges or media bias workshops.

Support campaigns that encourage transparency and accountability in journalism. Every conversation about media literacy empowers your community to think critically and act wisely.

Activism through Awareness

Activism isn't just about protests, rallies, or street slogans anymore. In the digital age, activism is about **awareness, education, and influence**.

You, as a member of Gen Z, have access to tools and platforms that make activism a collective and everyday effort. Social media, documentaries, podcasts, and storytelling are powerful avenues through which you can raise awareness, drive change, and create lasting social impact.

Activism through awareness means not only fighting for change but ensuring that people *understand why that change is necessary* and how they can contribute to it.

Social Media as a Tool for Education and Change

Social media isn't just a place to share memes, selfies, or dance videos. It's a dynamic platform where **education, awareness, and activism intersect**. Platforms like Instagram, TikTok, Twitter, and Facebook have become the frontline of social and political movements, where issues of climate change, social justice, mental health, and equality are discussed, debated, and brought to the forefront of global discourse.

Social media enables you to reach and educate people across the globe instantly. Movements like **#BlackLivesMatter, Fridays for Future, and MeToo** show how quickly ideas can spread, how solidarity can form, and how collective action can be organized.

Take **Instagram**. With its visuals and stories, you can share infographics explaining complex social issues, create reels that educate on climate science, or use IGTV to interview experts about mental health struggles. Similarly, **Twitter** serves as a platform for real-time updates, news sharing, and hashtags that amplify voices and demands globally.

But social media activism requires responsibility. It's crucial to:

1. **Verify Information**: Before you share a post, check the sources. Is it backed by credible evidence, studies, or experts? Share content that adds value and truth.
2. **Amplify Voices, Not Just Yourself**: Use your platform to elevate people who are marginalized or those with first-

hand experience. Share stories of those who often go unheard.

3. **Engage in Constructive Discussions**: Social media can be divisive. Use your influence to create conversations that educate, inform, and bridge divides rather than create echo chambers.

Social media activism **bridges global distances, builds solidarity, and turns followers into active participants**. It connects young people with experts, activists, and communities, transforming passive scrolling into active engagement and education.

Storytelling: A Powerful Tool

Storytelling is at the heart of meaningful activism. Stories create empathy, build connections, and inspire change far more effectively than facts and statistics alone.

When you tell stories about social issues, personal experiences, or community struggles, you humanize the challenges people face and connect your audience on a deeper emotional level.

A simple video showing the struggles of a local farmer dealing with climate change can spark awareness about sustainability. A personal account of mental health struggles can break down stigmas. These stories make issues tangible and relatable.

Storytelling is also about **sharing history and personal nar-**

ratives. When young people share stories about protests, climate strikes, or social justice initiatives, it becomes a tool of resistance and education.

Authenticity and vulnerability make storytelling impactful. When people share real experiences, struggles, and victories, it creates trust and inspires others to take action. Activism through awareness is about using the tools of storytelling, social media, documentaries, and podcasts not just to highlight issues but to ignite change.

It's about transforming passive audiences into informed, active participants who care about the world they live in and are ready to fight for it.

The future depends on your ability to amplify voices, question narratives, and drive meaningful conversations. Use social media, podcasts, documentaries, and stories to not only inform but also to activate and engage.

In doing so, you don't just create awareness—you drive action, shape conversations, and contribute to a movement that's about **real change, responsibility, and global solidarity**.

4

Embracing Activism and Purposeful Action

Action Over Words: Purpose-driven Change

Being a Gen Zer isn't just about having dreams or setting ambitious goals—it's about transforming those dreams into real, lasting impact through action and commitment.

Activism now requires more than just words and intentions; it demands a commitment to **systemic change, resilience**, and **deep, meaningful transformation**. It's about recognizing that every choice, every interaction, every project, and every platform you engage with has the potential to shape outcomes— not just for yourself, but for entire communities, ecosystems, and generations to come.

Activism Beyond the Obvious

Many people still think activism is about **protesting in the streets or rallying on social media**, but real progress stretches far beyond those visible acts. It's about a more **systemic, collaborative commitment to reshaping how society works**. It's challenging entrenched norms, dismantling inequities, and introducing new, sustainable, and inclusive solutions at every level.

Whether it's about **climate change, racial justice, gender equality, economic reform, or digital responsibility**, each effort should aim to make meaningful, long-term change that touches lives beyond superficial visibility.

Change is built through **policy reform, community initiatives**, and **innovative projects that address real-world problems head-on**. This means participating in **local governance, pushing for inclusive legislation**, and collaborating with community leaders who bring grassroots wisdom to the forefront.

It means contributing to **workshops, local councils, mentoring initiatives**, and **collective projects that empower communities from within** rather than offering short-term fixes from the outside.

Collaboration with Local Organizations and Social Enterprises

If you want to make a difference, work side-by-side with **local organizations and social enterprises**.

These groups often have the infrastructure and deep-rooted community ties that are essential for **long-term social and economic transformation**. Support initiatives that address issues like **education gaps, job accessibility**, and **environmental sustainability**. Volunteer your time, bring your expertise, or start your own initiatives that **blend purpose with profit and people-centric goals**.

Look into partnering with **startup projects that focus on social impact**, businesses that practice ethical sourcing, or community-driven initiatives that aim to uplift marginalized groups. These collaborations aren't just about **financial transactions**; they're about **knowledge exchange, empowerment**, and **sustaining community efforts**.

Commitment Beyond Visibility

Social media and protests are crucial tools to raise awareness and gather support, but **sustainable change is embedded in commitment and continuity**. It comes through **consistent community engagement, education campaigns**, and **projects that grow stronger over time**.

Whether it's organizing a local food drive, starting a community clean-up, or collaborating with schools to introduce sustainability education—these initiatives lay the foundation for resilient communities and long-term progress.

Use your creativity and technological skills to launch initiatives that solve real-world problems. Build apps that promote **local volunteering**, create **online platforms for knowledge-sharing**, or use data-driven tools to optimize **environmental sustainability projects**.

A Deeper Purpose-Driven Commitment

True activism, as a Gen Zer, means committing your resources—time, creativity, skills, and finances—to causes that resonate deeply with your values. It's about dedicating yourself to **causes that fight inequality, protect the environment, support digital responsibility**, and **ensure transparency and fairness in corporate practices**.

Ask yourself:

- How can your skills contribute to **community sustainability projects**?
- What initiatives can you support that tackle **systemic inequalities head-on**?
- How can your voice amplify **marginalized communities**, and how do you bring diversity and inclusivity to leadership roles?

This commitment should be **authentic, scalable, and adaptable**, capable of growing and transforming alongside the challenges it aims to address.

Being a Gen Zer means transforming your passions into purpose, your creativity into tools for change, and your commitment into a legacy that **elevates collective responsibility, builds resilience**, and **pushes society toward a future of equality, sustainability**, and **genuine social progress**.

Every choice you make today—whether through your business practices, your voting habits, your collaborations, or your daily interactions—should contribute to a society that isn't just successful but **inclusive, sustainable**, and **committed to the well-being of every individual, community, and future generation**.

Purpose-driven Activism Goes Beyond Short-Term Goals

Transforming ideas into action means engaging in initiatives that create **long-term systemic change** and uplift communities. This isn't about quick fixes; it's about building projects, infrastructure, and support systems that create sustainable opportunities and resilience.

Whether it's in **education, agriculture, waste management**, or **corporate responsibility**, every effort should focus on strengthening communities, empowering individuals, and fostering self-sufficiency.

Education Initiatives That Empower and Equip

Education should not just teach facts—it should cultivate **critical thinking, adaptability, and resilience**. Start initiatives that bring practical education into schools, teaching **real-world skills like financial literacy, coding, environmental sustainability**, and **emotional intelligence**.

Work with local schools to integrate **practical workshops, peer mentoring, and community projects** into the curriculum.

Support mentorship platforms for underprivileged youth, where young professionals and students can share **career advice, skill-building workshops**, and **real-world experiences**.

Collaborate with nonprofits, local businesses, and professionals to provide internships and job opportunities.

The goal is to make sure that education becomes a tool for upward mobility, **equipping young people with the skills to drive change in their communities**, not just their personal lives.

Supporting Local Farmers and Sustainable Agriculture

Sustaining communities also means prioritizing **local food systems and agriculture**. Support local farmers by creating initiatives that connect farms with schools, community markets, and local restaurants. Promote **community-supported agriculture (CSA) programs**, encourage urban farming projects, and work on initiatives that reduce food waste.

Introduce sustainable farming practices, share knowledge about **composting, organic farming, and crop rotation**, and work on projects that integrate **environmental sustainability into agriculture**.

Help create infrastructure that supports **local production, distribution**, and **eco-friendly farming practices**, ensuring food security and boosting local economies.

Recycling Projects and Waste Reduction Initiatives

Address environmental challenges through **community recycling projects and waste reduction initiatives**. Start campaigns that educate communities about proper waste disposal, composting, and **circular economy practices**, where waste is transformed into valuable resources.

Implement projects that focus on **plastic reduction, e-waste recycling**, and **upcycling initiatives**, turning what others discard into useful tools, art, and infrastructure.

Partner with local businesses to encourage **zero-waste practices and eco-friendly packaging**. Advocate for policies that mandate companies to take responsibility for their product lifecycle, ensuring that products are either **recyclable, compostable**, or **reusable**, minimizing environmental impact.

Corporate Responsibility and Sustainable Business Models

Push companies to move beyond token efforts and embed **social responsibility and sustainability into their core values**. Advocate for transparency in corporate practices, where **ethics, fairness**, and **accountability** aren't just statements on websites but integral aspects of business operations. Support businesses that commit to **sustainable production lines, ethical sourcing**, and **environmentally conscious operations**.

Encourage companies to adopt **fair trade certifications**, prioritize **worker rights**, and invest in **employee well-being initiatives**. Advocate for corporate models that focus on **long-term community engagement, profit sharing**, and **corporate social responsibility (CSR) projects** that bring tangible benefits to communities rather than just superficial contributions.

Community Infrastructure That Lasts

Commit to projects that bring **lasting infrastructure improvements to communities**.

This could include **building community centers, improving public transportation**, creating **green spaces**, and developing **affordable housing projects** that use eco-friendly materials and sustainable construction methods. Infrastructure projects should be about building **resilience, accessibility**, and **long-term sustainability**, ensuring that communities have the support systems they need to thrive for generations.

Work alongside local governments, nonprofits, and community members to prioritize projects that bring **employment opportunities, skill development**, and **social infrastructure**, creating spaces where people can collaborate, innovate, and grow together.

A Collective Commitment to Social Impact

Every initiative should have a commitment to **social impact, environmental sustainability**, and **economic fairness**. It's about creating a culture where **profit isn't at the expense of people or the planet**. Every product sold, every service offered, every decision made should reflect a commitment to **social equity, community support**, and **environmental responsibility**.

By committing to projects and initiatives that focus on **education, agriculture, waste reduction, corporate transparency**, and **community development**, Gen Z can drive a movement that prioritizes **long-term solutions, real-world impact**, and **collective well-being**.

This commitment isn't about fleeting trends—it's about laying the foundation for a society where sustainability, ethics, and equity are not aspirations but norms woven into the fabric of every decision, every project, and every interaction.

Leveraging Technology for Social Impact

Technology is not just a means of convenience or entertainment—it should be a powerful force for **empowerment, education**, and **social progress**. As digital natives, you have the skills, insights, and creativity to use technology as a tool that tackles real-world problems, bridges gaps, and elevates communities.

Every line of code, every app developed, every social media post should reflect a commitment to **purpose-driven progress**, social impact, and collective good.

Empowerment Through Purpose-Driven Tools

Consider building **apps and platforms that serve a purpose beyond profit**. Create tools that facilitate **local volunteering**, connect people with mentorship opportunities, or offer **educational resources tailored to underprivileged communities**.

Think about AI-driven initiatives that personalize learning experiences for students who need extra support, or platforms that enable **lifelong skill development**, preparing young people for careers that are both meaningful and in demand.

Technology should also be a force that connects resources with needs. Develop platforms where **pro bono services, knowledge sharing, donations**, and community support become seamless. Whether someone needs free legal advice, digital marketing skills, or mental health resources, these tools should break down barriers and provide **access to expertise, support, and opportunity**, ensuring that no one is left behind.

Social Media with Substance, Not Just Style

Social media platforms are powerful tools for change, but they often prioritize **superficial trends and consumer culture**. It's time to push these platforms to be **tools for meaningful engagement, transparency**, and **critical discourse**. Demand features that go beyond likes and follower counts—features that promote **constructive dialogue, fact-checking mechanisms**, and **transparency algorithms**.

Call for social media companies to introduce **tools that support mental health, reduce screen addiction**, and encourage **positive interactions** rather than promoting fleeting entertainment.

Encourage platforms to highlight stories of **climate action, social justice efforts, and grassroots initiatives**, giving visibility to causes that matter rather than fleeting celebrity news or viral trends.

Using Your Voice to Educate and Mobilize

Leverage social media as a vehicle for **education and mobilization**, not just consumption. Use your digital presence to discuss **climate change solutions, racial equity**, and **gender inclusivity**.

Share stories of resilience and solidarity, collaborate on initiatives that address social issues, and use your platforms to **high-light voices that are often unheard**—those of marginalized communities, differently-abled individuals, and underrepresented groups.

Start or support **online campaigns that push for policy change, corporate accountability**, and **transparency in data usage**. Whether it's a tweet thread about **sustainable practices in tech companies, a viral challenge promoting inclusivity**, or a collaborative video discussing **social responsibility**, your digital engagement should focus on **impact and education**, sparking real conversations that extend offline.

AI and Technology as Tools for Social Good

Embrace AI and machine learning not just for efficiency, but as instruments of **social good and equity**. Develop algorithms that prioritize **fairness, transparency**, and **ethical decision-making**. Challenge biases that perpetuate social inequality in AI systems, advocate for **inclusive datasets**, and collaborate on technologies that represent a diverse and realistic world.

Artificial intelligence can be a tool that amplifies diverse voices, builds empathy, and addresses systemic issues, but it must be **trained and deployed with responsibility and care**.

Support startups and projects that focus on **AI-driven social solutions**, such as tools for **mental health support, community engagement**, and **accessible education**. Create AI models that empower rather than exploit, that heal rather than divide, and that uplift rather than isolate.

A Generation of Digital Responsibility

Being a digital generation means embracing a commitment to **ethical tech use, transparency**, and **social responsibility**. Every interaction online should reflect your commitment to **sustainability, equity**, and **community support**.

Support and collaborate with companies that align with these values—those that prioritize **renewable energy use, fair trade sourcing**, and **corporate social responsibility**.

Call for greater accountability in tech companies, demanding transparency about **data privacy policies, algorithmic decision-making**, and **supply chain practices**. Push for policies that mandate **fair wages, employee rights**, and **environmentally conscious business practices**, ensuring that technology serves humanity, not just profits.

Technology should serve as a tool for **empowerment, education, social progress**, and **environmental stewardship**. As a generation that understands the intricacies of the digital landscape better than any before, you have the responsibility—and the power—to create a digital world that **uplifts everyone, protects the environment**, and **nurtures equality and transparency**.

Use technology not just to innovate but to **transform, to heal, to educate**, and most importantly, to create a world where progress is measured by **well-being, resilience**, and **shared**

prosperity, not just clicks and views.

Inclusivity and Solidarity as a Basis for True Change

Real activism isn't about performance—it's about impact, solidarity, and transformation. It's about creating a world where systemic barriers are dismantled, where opportunities are open to all, and where every voice, regardless of race, gender, socioeconomic background, or ability, is heard, respected, and uplifted.

True activism requires a commitment to **justice, equality**, and **community well-being** at every level.

A Commitment to Genuine Solidarity

Solidarity means more than standing together; it's about **actively supporting, listening**, and **working alongside communities that have been historically marginalized**. It means ensuring that activism doesn't just shine a spotlight on problems but addresses them **through sustained efforts and tangible solutions**.

This could mean partnering with local organizations to address issues of **income disparity, racial injustice**, and **gender inequality**, or supporting initiatives that create **affordable housing, accessible healthcare**, and **educational opportunities**.

Support marginalized communities by recognizing their

strengths and leadership. Empower voices that have often been silenced and uplift local leaders who come from these communities. Whether you're advocating for **Indigenous rights, supporting differently-abled communities**, or fighting for **racial and gender equity**, your role is to amplify these voices—not just out of solidarity but out of respect, understanding, and accountability.

Listening and Learning First

Engage with communities not just as an activist but as a **listener and a learner**. The most effective change comes when activism is rooted in understanding the lived experiences of those you aim to support. This means stepping back and **asking questions instead of making assumptions**, actively participating in **community forums**, and creating initiatives that are shaped by **input from those directly affected**.

Initiatives should prioritize **mutual knowledge sharing, collaboration**, and **respect-based support systems**. Let leadership be about **empowering others**, fostering opportunities for people to step into leadership roles themselves, and prioritizing **collective progress** over **individual advancement**. When you uplift someone, you uplift a community.

When you support a local project, you strengthen bonds that ripple through the entire community.

Building Inclusive Opportunities

True activism creates opportunities that are accessible to everyone, no matter their race, gender, socioeconomic status, or ability. This could mean organizing initiatives where **education and job training are freely accessible**, where **technology is designed for inclusivity**, and where **public spaces are accessible to everyone**.

Make sure that initiatives are not just about inclusion in name but reflect true accessibility, equity, and respect in **implementation and results**.

Incorporate **adaptive technologies and multilingual education systems** that address the unique challenges of differently-abled individuals and non-native speakers. Support projects that **create jobs for marginalized communities**, not just in positions of labor but in leadership and decision-making roles as well.

Every job should come with **fair wages, respect, and the possibility for advancement**.

Policy Change and Grassroots Commitment

Support and drive **policy reforms that protect civil rights, prioritize social equity, and champion economic fairness**. Grassroots activism must align with policies that ensure **transparency in governance, fair trade practices, and corporate accountability**.

Whether it's pushing for **environmental protection laws**, advocating for **social equity reforms**, or supporting **transparent political candidates**, your activism should seek long-term systemic change.

Collaborating with local leaders, policymakers, and organizations allows you to build campaigns that influence not only **public opinion but also policy**, ensuring that systemic change is embedded into the foundation of local and national frameworks.

Action Rooted in Respect and Cooperation

Every action should be about **respect, cooperation**, and **building trust**. Work together with people from different walks of life to brainstorm, plan, and execute initiatives that focus on community betterment. Leadership should be about **serving others rather than self-promotion**, about empowering others to take charge, to innovate, and to lead their communities with purpose.

Stand alongside your community members, **celebrating diversity, tackling inequality**, and **creating solutions that leave no one behind**. Encourage projects where profits and proceeds go back into the community rather than just enriching a few individuals. Whether it's **community gardening initiatives, local cooperatives**, or **mentorship programs**, these projects should uplift everyone, making **social and economic sustainability** the core objective.

Activism today is about creating realities where solidarity

isn't a slogan but a lived experience. It's about ensuring that everyone has access to **opportunities, education**, and **justice**, driven by a commitment to **equity, transparency**, and **lasting social impact**.

As a member of Gen Z, you aren't just continuing the work of past generations—you're shaping a new, inclusive reality where **every person thrives, every community flourishes**, and **change is not only achieved but also sustained** by care, responsibility, and collective action.

Education as a Gateway to Empowerment

Education shouldn't just be about memorizing facts and passing tests. It should be a **tool for real-world transformation**, a foundation for critical thinking, and a launchpad for social responsibility and collaborative entrepreneurship.

True education empowers young people not only with knowledge but also with the **skills, ethics, and adaptability needed to drive change, solve problems**, and **build resilient communities**.

Emphasizing Critical Thinking Over Memorization

A curriculum focused on **critical thinking and problem-solving** means encouraging students to question, analyze, and evaluate information rather than just absorb it. Schools should prioritize **discussion-based learning, debates**, and **group projects** that encourage dialogue, disagreement, and resolution. It's about fostering curiosity and empowering students to think independently and strategically.

Incorporating subjects like **logic, philosophy, and critical analysis** alongside traditional sciences and literature teaches students to ask meaningful questions. Why do things work the way they do? How do choices impact society, the environment, or the economy? These questions lead to **deeper engagement, introspection**, and **decision-making skills**.

Real-World Problem Solving and Social Responsibility

We need school curriculums to address **real-world challenges** by including subjects and projects that teach **financial literacy, sustainability, social sciences**, and **civic responsibility**. A student who understands **personal finance, environmental impact**, and **social ethics** is better equipped to contribute positively to society. Lessons in **budgeting, saving, investments**, and **basic economics** should be as standard as learning multiplication or grammar.

Moreover, include modules on **social responsibility and civic engagement**, which teach young people about voting, community service, activism, and advocacy.

How does local policy affect communities?

How do social issues connect to economic disparities or climate change?

This knowledge empowers students to become **active citizens**, equipped to make informed decisions and drive initiatives that address **inequality, poverty**, and **climate challenges**.

Practical Skills for Adaptability and Life Readiness

Education should focus on **practical skills that prepare students for life beyond school**. This means prioritizing **career-oriented knowledge, digital literacy, and communication skills** alongside academic subjects. Schools should encourage programs like **coding workshops, entrepreneurship boot camps**, and **practical science labs** that emphasize real-world application rather than theoretical knowledge alone.

Support initiatives that teach **soft skills like teamwork, resilience**, and **emotional intelligence**. These are just as critical as technical knowledge because success in the real world depends on **communication, adaptability**, and **collaborative leadership**. Group activities, interactive workshops, and peer mentoring programs should become a norm rather than an exception.

Moving Education Beyond the Classroom Walls

Support initiatives that extend learning beyond textbooks and traditional classrooms. Real-world internships, community projects, and peer mentoring should be integrated into the core educational experience. These initiatives allow students to **gain hands-on experience**, interact with professionals across fields, and collaborate with peers from different backgrounds.

For example, a student might participate in **a local community cleanup project, work with startups through internships**, or engage in **peer-to-peer educational initiatives where knowledge sharing becomes a two-way street**.

Such projects offer **insight into real challenges, collaborative problem-solving**, and the power of **community engagement and leadership**.

Collaborative Entrepreneurship and Ethical Leadership

Education should also nurture **entrepreneurial skills and leadership ethics**. Teach students how to create **social enterprises, start cooperatives**, and run initiatives that aim for **profit with purpose**, focusing on **community benefit and social impact**.

Encourage schools to partner with **local businesses, startups**, and **non-profits**, offering opportunities where students can contribute, learn, and innovate.

Leadership education should instill a commitment to **ethical decision-making, transparency**, and **corporate social responsibility**. Future leaders should learn that business success isn't just about profit—it's about **creating value for people, the environment**, and **communities**, ensuring long-term sustainability.

Empowerment Through Adaptability and Innovation

Ultimately, education should be about **empowering students with adaptability and resilience**, preparing them not just for academic success but for the realities of life, work, and change.

In a world where **technological advances, climate challenges, and social dynamics evolve rapidly**, young people need to learn how to **adapt, innovate**, and **rethink systems quickly and thoughtfully**.

Support **curriculums that focus on lifelong learning skills, adaptability, creativity**, and **self-driven exploration**, teaching students that progress and innovation come from a mindset of curiosity, resilience, and a commitment to continuous improvement.

Education for real change means preparing young people not just to survive but to thrive, contribute, and transform society sustainably. It's about equipping each student with a clear understanding of **critical thinking, ethical responsibility**, and **practical adaptability**, ensuring that every new generation becomes a force that not only dreams but also builds, reforms, and uplifts.

5

Leading Ethical Innovation and Technological Integrity

Redefining Progress with Purpose

Technology has transformed the world in ways that once seemed unimaginable. But progress is no longer just about building faster machines, scaling massive operations, or reaching millions of users overnight.

It's about **purpose, responsibility**, and **human-centric design**. It's about making sure that every technological advance serves not just profit-driven goals but a broader commitment to **community well-being, environmental sustainability**, and **social equity**.

As Gen Z, you're not just consumers of technology; you're its architects, critics, and decision-makers. You have the power to drive innovation in ways that center **people, purpose**, and

planet, prioritizing collective good over short-term gains.

Every choice you make in tech—every line of code, every feature, every user interface—has consequences. These aren't just business decisions; they are **social choices** and **moral commitments**. Consider how your work affects **communities, ecosystems, and individual lives**.

Ask yourself deeper questions: Is this product solving a real problem, or just creating new ones? Does it contribute to social equity, or does it reinforce systemic inequalities? Is it accessible to everyone, regardless of ability, race, or socioeconomic status? Does it foster trust, respect privacy, and maintain transparency, or does it exploit data and spread misinformation?

Technological progress should never come at the expense of **environmental degradation, exploitation**, or **social inequity**. It shouldn't be a force that deepens divides, fuels misinformation, or encourages wasteful consumption. Instead, progress should be a powerful tool that **educates, connects, and elevates**. A tool that empowers individuals with knowledge, fosters collective creativity, and builds sustainable communities.

Technology should be about **creating solutions that endure**, not just quick fixes that disappear as fast as trends change.

Consider the environmental impact of every digital decision. Every piece of hardware contributes to **e-waste**, every data center generates **carbon emissions**, and every online transaction consumes energy. What if technology didn't contribute to these problems but solved them? What if products were made from

sustainable materials, software was optimized to reduce energy consumption, and companies prioritized **circular economies** where waste is minimized, and every component is reused or recycled?

Look at social responsibility through the lens of **equitable access**. Millions of people around the world still lack access to reliable internet, quality education, or affordable tech. Your role as a tech-savvy generation is to design systems that **bridge gaps**, rather than widen them.

Develop tools that empower **rural communities**, support **educational equity**, and offer **opportunities for skill development**, ensuring that everyone has a chance to succeed in a digital world. Push for platforms and apps that prioritize **transparency, consent**, and **data protection**, not just functionality and profit.

You have the chance to redefine **corporate responsibility**. Support businesses that align with your values, companies that embrace **fair labor practices, environmental stewardship**, and **corporate transparency**. Demand that these companies don't just follow sustainability trends but drive them. Consider entrepreneurship as an avenue to create startups that operate with **integrity, purpose**, and **long-term commitment to sustainability**, ensuring that profits are tied to **social impact**, not just shareholder value.

At its core, technological progress should be a force that **educates minds, strengthens communities**, and **restores the environment**. It should connect people instead of isolating them, foster creativity rather than conformity, and build resilience rather than dependency. It should be about creating a **digital landscape where ideas flourish, collaboration is seamless**, and **every individual has the tools and opportunities to contribute meaningfully** to society.

Ultimately, your role in shaping technology is about committing to a vision of progress that serves **people, respects the planet**, and **uplifts society**. Progress should be a commitment to **transparency, sustainability, equity**, and **human dignity**. Every decision you make in tech should be a reflection of these values. As you drive innovation, remember that you're not just building technology—you're building **trust, resilience**, and **a future where progress benefits everyone, not just a select few**.

Accountability in the Digital Space

The digital world offers incredible opportunities but comes with its own set of challenges.

You see it every day—**data privacy breaches, algorithmic bias**, misinformation spreading like wildfire, and a growing sense of **social isolation**. As the digital generation, you don't just use technology; you *shape* it, and with that comes the responsibility to demand accountability from those who create, distribute, and profit from it—**tech companies, social platforms**, and **content creators**. Transparent policies, fair algorithms, and ethical data handling shouldn't be optional; they need to be the **baseline standard**.

Data privacy is a critical battleground. Every click, search, and interaction feeds into complex data systems that can either empower or compromise privacy. Data breaches aren't just inconveniences; they're invasions of trust. Demand that tech companies have clear, accessible policies on **data usage**, **storage**, and **sharing**. Support initiatives that push for **end-to-end encryption, user consent**, and **strong data protection measures**.

Encourage social platforms to prioritize privacy settings that are **clear, actionable**, and **respect user autonomy**, rather than burying them in confusing terms of service.

Algorithmic bias is another issue that requires urgent attention. Algorithms aren't neutral; they reflect the data and biases that shape them. Whether it's **recommendation systems, hiring tools**, or **facial recognition software**, biases can reinforce **discrimination, inequality**, and **injustice**.

As Gen Z, you have the expertise and perspective to **audit, analyze**, and **question these systems**. Advocate for algorithmic transparency—companies should be open about how their algorithms work, what data they use, and the steps taken to mitigate bias. Support startups and tech initiatives that prioritize **fairness, inclusivity**, and **representation** in their design and implementation.

The spread of **misinformation** on social media platforms further compounds these challenges. Whether it's fake news, deepfakes, or unverified health claims, misinformation can have real-world consequences. Demand accountability from social platforms to implement **effective content moderation, fact-checking mechanisms**, and **AI tools** that reduce harmful disinformation.

Support creators and influencers who prioritize **truth, transparency**, and **critical discourse** rather than just likes and virality. Promote digital literacy in schools and communities—educate people on **source verification, media bias**, and **critical thinking**.

Social isolation is a more subtle but equally harmful result of the digital landscape. Platforms that should bring people together often create echo chambers and filter bubbles, isolating users from diverse perspectives and meaningful interactions. Push for social media designs that **foster engagement, diversity of thought**, and **real-world connections**. Support tech initiatives that encourage **offline interactions, mental health awareness**, and **community-building activities**. Demand features that prioritize **well-being**—like time management tools, mental health reminders, and **balance indicators** that help users maintain a healthy relationship with technology.

Support companies that demonstrate **transparency and ethical conduct**. This means prioritizing **corporate social responsibility, fair labor practices**, and **environmental sustainability**. If you're considering a job or supporting a brand, evaluate their commitment to **employee well-being, environmental stewardship**, and **community impact**. Demand that these companies don't just adopt **superficial sustainability measures** but integrate them into every facet of their operations.

As an innovator, advocate, and consumer, you have the opportunity to drive real change. Work with startups that focus on **social impact, digital well-being**, and **ethical technology**.

Partner with organizations that align with your commitment to **transparency, accountability**, and **social responsibility**. Use your voice to **call out harmful practices**, support initiatives that build **trust, inclusivity**, and **community resilience**, and push for tech that serves not just profit but **people, purpose**, and **planet**.

Demand accountability not just from tech companies, but from **content creators, influencers**, and **the digital communities you participate in**. Promote a culture of **critical thinking, transparency**, and **ethical engagement**—because responsible tech use and development aren't just about good business or good design; they're about **creating a digital world that builds trust, empowers communities**, and **uplifts everyone, everywhere**.

Inclusive Design: Tech for Everyone

Innovation should never be limited to a select few. It should be about empowering **everyone, everywhere**, regardless of age, race, gender, ability, or background. Inclusive technology design is about creating tools that are accessible, adaptable, and empowering—tools that don't just serve a privileged segment of society but uplift **entire communities, cultures**, and **individual experiences**. This means focusing on **accessibility features,**

multilingual interfaces, and **adaptive technologies** that meet the needs of people from all walks of life.

Right now, many tech companies fall short when it comes to inclusive design. Too often, the needs of **differently-abled individuals**, **marginalized communities**, and **underrepresented groups** are overlooked or only considered as an afterthought.

Whether it's an app without proper voice navigation features, a website that fails accessibility guidelines, or a social media platform that doesn't accommodate language diversity, these oversights reflect a broader issue of exclusion in design thinking.

But this is where **you, Gen Z**, step in. You have the creativity, knowledge, and empathy to drive change. Your generation has grown up immersed in diverse cultures, experiences, and perspectives. You understand firsthand that **technology should empower, not isolate**, and that innovation is at its best when it serves a wider, richer community of users.

Inclusive design means prioritizing **simple, functional accessibility options**. It means incorporating features like **text-to-speech, closed captions**, and **color contrast adjustments**, ensuring that every interface and experience is usable for those with visual, auditory, or motor challenges.

It also means thinking about **language diversity** by creating multilingual interfaces and content that reflect the multilingual realities of global communities. Design products that seamlessly work across cultures, languages, and abilities—not just in your local community but on a global scale.

This approach should be more than just a checkbox or compliance requirement. It should be a core principle in every product decision and development process. Advocate for tech companies to adopt **web accessibility standards**, follow **WCAG (Web Content Accessibility Guidelines)**, and prioritize **user-centric design principles**. Support and work with startups that are committed to building technology for social good, prioritizing **environmental sustainability**, **digital literacy**, and **economic inclusiveness**.

Push for **educational initiatives in schools and communities** that teach inclusive coding, adaptive design principles, and accessibility best practices. Learn from designers and developers with disabilities, marginalized voices, and underserved communities. Their insights will shape technology in ways that go beyond mere functionality—they will bring about **resilient, adaptable, and community-focused solutions**.

Technology, at its best, should be a tool for **connection, empowerment**, and **community growth**. Build apps that don't just serve profit-driven goals but actively improve lives. Create software that strengthens communities rather than dividing them. Design products that **uplift every user experience**, celebrate diversity, and ensure no one is left out of technological progress.

As the next generation of thinkers, creators, and leaders, you have the chance to define a future where innovation means **inclusivity, accessibility**, and **social responsibility**. Make tech that serves **all backgrounds, all abilities**, and all voices—not just in word, but in action.

Build, code, innovate—not just with profit in mind, but with a commitment to creating a world where technology is a bridge that connects, empowers, and elevates **everyone, everywhere**.

Sustainable Technology: A Commitment to the Planet

Sustainability isn't just a moral ideal—it's a requirement for survival and progress. Every tech innovation, every new device, and every production line choice carries an environmental footprint, whether it's through **electronic waste, carbon emissions**, or **resource extraction**. As the generation driving technology forward, you hold the responsibility to ensure that innovation doesn't come at the expense of **planet health** or **environmental stability**.

Your work should prioritize **green solutions, eco-friendly design**, and **sustainable practices**.

Every technological breakthrough has an environmental trade-off. Electronics contain hazardous materials that often end up in landfills, contaminating soil and water. The energy-intensive manufacturing processes contribute significantly to **carbon emissions**, while poor sourcing practices deplete **natural resources** and harm **biodiversity**. But you have the power to change these dynamics.

Start by **advocating for sustainable production methods**. Support companies committed to **renewable energy sourcing**, **minimal waste production**, and **closed-loop manufacturing**. Encourage brands to adopt circular economies, where products are **recycled, refurbished**, and **resold**, reducing the need for raw materials and minimizing waste. Look for companies that prioritize **eco-conscious sourcing of materials**, ensuring that every resource, from metals to textiles, is responsibly and ethically obtained.

Promote initiatives focused on **electronic recycling programs**. Tech waste is growing at an alarming rate—over **50 million tons annually worldwide**. Encourage community recycling centers and online initiatives where people can donate or recycle old electronics. Participate in or organize **e-waste collection drives**, where schools, communities, and workplaces come together to safely dispose of electronics.

When developing your projects or collaborating with others, make eco-friendly choices a priority. Consider the energy efficiency of your technology choices and choose **low-energy hardware and software solutions**. Optimize code to be more resource-efficient, ensuring that digital products consume less energy. Factor in how your choices impact **supply chain logistics**, transportation emissions, and material sourcing.

Work on projects that focus on **clean energy integration**, such as solar-powered devices, energy-efficient servers, or apps promoting eco-friendly transportation. Incorporating sustainability into your digital design means creating interfaces and applications that encourage **sustainable consumer behavior**, like energy-saving reminders or eco-friendly lifestyle trackers.

Sustainability is about integrating these principles into every step of innovation—every code line, design choice, and marketing strategy should reflect a commitment to **environmental responsibility**.

As the next generation, use your creativity and influence to drive policies that mandate **eco-friendly corporate practices**, push governments to invest in **clean technology infrastructure**, and demand transparency about **environmental impact** from tech companies.

Remember, **sustainable tech** is not just about preserving the environment—it's about **equitable growth, social responsibility**, and **community resilience**. When we innovate with sustainability in mind, we lay the foundation for a future where technology acts as a force that **nourishes, connects**, and **sustains**, rather than depletes.

Every choice you make as a creator, consumer, and leader should contribute to a system where **technology, people**, and the **planet coexist in balance**.

Drive change by creating, advocating, and building not just for profit but for a **planet that thrives, communities that flourish**, and a world that remains **resilient, inclusive**, and **sustainable for generations to come**.

Ethics as a Foundation for Innovation

Technology should be a tool for **empowerment, education**, and **connection**, not division or misinformation. It's about building tools that foster **critical thinking, education**, and **community engagement**. This means developing platforms and apps that encourage **learning, creativity**, and **collaboration** instead of mindless consumption or superficial interactions.

Push for **transparency in algorithms, honest content curation**, and **educational technologies** that focus on **skill development, critical inquiry**, and **long-term knowledge retention**. Encourage platforms and companies to adopt **fair algorithms** that are free from bias and promote **equitable exposure** to diverse cultures and perspectives.

The Role of Young Leaders in Shaping Tomorrow

You are not just users of technology—you are its leaders, designers, and critics. Whether you're **starting a tech company, joining a digital team**, or **creating content**, your role is to shape tech that serves a greater good. You have the power to drive **purpose-driven startups**, contribute to **innovative projects**, and influence tech policies that prioritize **social good** and **community welfare**.

Leadership in technology is about more than profit margins; it's about purpose, resilience, and impact. Create work cultures and companies where **sustainability**, **diversity**, and **employee well-being** are core values. Work environments should be places where people **thrive, innovate**, and **contribute positively** to society.

A Future Built on Ethical Progress

Ethical innovation is not an idealistic vision—it's a practical choice with real-world implications. Every decision you make shapes **your community, your environment**, and **the global landscape**. Change starts with small, conscious choices: creating **accessible software**, supporting **eco-friendly startups**, participating in **open-source projects**, and advocating for **digital literacy and transparency**.

As Gen Z, your commitment to **ethical innovation** and **social responsibility** will ripple through industries, cultures, and generations. It will set the foundation for a future where technology is a force for **good, sustainability**, and **progress that benefits everyone, not just a select few**.

By prioritizing ethics in your work, supporting sustainable and inclusive initiatives, and fostering transparency and accountability, you're not just shaping technology—you're building a society that values **integrity, responsibility**, and **lasting progress for all**.

6

Embracing Diversity – Building Strength in Unity

Understanding Diversity and Inclusion

Diversity is not about superficial efforts—it's about **genuine engagement, curiosity**, and **valuing every individual's experiences and perspectives**. In today's interconnected world, diversity goes beyond race and gender; it includes **socioeconomic status, culture, abilities, experiences**, and **belief systems**.

Embracing diversity means recognizing the richness that different backgrounds and experiences bring to our personal lives, communities, workplaces, and even our social interactions.

The Significance of Diversity in an Interconnected World

Many Gen Z individuals have had early exposure to diversity through **social media, global news, multicultural schools**, and **diverse neighborhoods**. This exposure offers a broader worldview but should be seen as just the starting point.

Real engagement with diversity requires moving beyond the surface and embracing **the stories, struggles, and strengths of people from different backgrounds**.

- **Listening with Curiosity:** Ask questions, share experiences, and genuinely engage with people whose lives and viewpoints differ from yours.
- **Continuous Learning:** Seek to understand cultures, experiences, and challenges different from your own. Attend workshops, read books, or participate in community initiatives where diverse perspectives are highlighted.

Studies have shown that organizations that prioritize diversity experience better teamwork, innovation, and problem-solving (Harvard Business Review, 2019). Diversity brings together different viewpoints, allowing for **creative problem-solving and deeper understanding**.

Inclusion: From Diversity to Action

Inclusion is where diversity shifts from a concept into a practical commitment. It's about creating environments where **everyone's voice is valued, and every individual has an equal opportunity to contribute and succeed**.

- **Actively Listen:** Inclusion means encouraging everyone to share their thoughts and experiences without fear of being ignored or dismissed.
- **Challenge Your Own Biases:** Reflect on personal biases and challenge assumptions. Ask yourself, *"Am I listening to everyone equally?"* or *"Am I only hearing viewpoints that align with my own experiences?"*
- **Support Inclusive Initiatives:** Participate in events, groups, or initiatives that promote diverse leadership, mentorship, and cross-cultural engagement.

Studies by the American Psychological Association highlight that inclusive workplaces and communities foster **higher satisfaction, creativity**, and **a stronger sense of purpose** (APA, 2018).

Diversity as a Source of Strength

Every person carries a unique story, background, and experience that can contribute to a collective effort in meaningful ways. Recognizing this means valuing **different viewpoints,**

backgrounds, cultures, and **life experiences**.

- **Innovation and Creativity:** Different experiences bring fresh ideas and unique solutions. Diverse teams are known to produce more creative outcomes because they offer a wider range of perspectives and skills (McKinsey & Company, 2020).
- **Community Resilience:** Communities that embrace diversity tend to be **more adaptable, empathetic**, and **capable of addressing challenges collectively**.
- **Personal Growth:** Interacting with people from various backgrounds not only broadens your understanding of the world but also enhances **emotional intelligence, patience**, and **communication skills**.

For example, multicultural experiences often improve cross-cultural communication, a skill that is increasingly valuable in workplaces and global interactions.

Practical Ways to Foster Diversity and Inclusion

- **Collaborate with Diverse Groups:** Work on projects that involve people from different cultures, disciplines, and backgrounds.
- **Support Education Initiatives:** Participate in or contribute to initiatives that educate young people about diversity, inclusion, and social justice.
- **Amplify Marginalized Voices:** Use your platforms—social media, community groups, workplaces—to highlight stories, projects, and voices from people who are often over-

looked.

Studies show that initiatives that promote diversity and inclusion not only contribute positively to individuals' mental health but also strengthen organizational loyalty, commitment, and community engagement.

Diversity is about engaging with the richness of different experiences rather than just tolerating differences. Inclusion is not a passive effort; it requires action, openness, and a commitment to creating spaces where everyone feels respected, heard, and empowered.

Embracing diversity strengthens relationships, fuels creativity, and builds resilience in communities, workplaces, and beyond. In a diverse world, every experience and perspective adds value—fostering resilience, adaptability, and progress in all aspects of life.

By engaging authentically with diversity and inclusion, you contribute to creating environments that are not just **effective, resilient**, but also **empathetic and adaptable**—qualities that will shape your success, creativity, and purpose-driven endeavors for years to come.

Communicating Across Differences

Communication is the foundation of connection, but **communicating across cultures, backgrounds, and experiences** requires more intention and respect. Misunderstandings often stem from **assumptions, stereotypes**, or a lack of exposure to diverse perspectives. Being mindful and deliberate in communication can turn these challenges into opportunities for connection, understanding, and growth.

Active Listening: The Heart of Effective Communication

Active listening is not just hearing words—it's about **engaging fully with the speaker, understanding their message**, and responding thoughtfully.

- **Focus Entirely on the Speaker:** Put away distractions. Maintain eye contact, nod in acknowledgment, and use verbal affirmations like *"I see," "That makes sense,"* or *"Tell me more."*
- **Clarify and Confirm Understanding:** Ask questions to clear up confusion, such as *"Could you share more about that experience?"* or *"I want to make sure I understand what you meant by...?"*
- **Reflect Back What You Hear:** Summarizing the speaker's points shows that you value their input and ensures mutual clarity. For example, *"So what I hear you saying is...?"*

Research supports that active listening builds trust, reduces

conflict, and fosters stronger relationships (Harvard Business Review, 2017). People are more likely to communicate openly when they feel heard and understood.

Embracing Openness: Asking Questions Instead of Making Assumptions

Many misunderstandings occur because we assume we already understand someone's experiences, opinions, or intentions. This assumption-driven communication often leads to mistakes and missed connections.

- **Ask Open-Ended Questions:** Questions like *"What are your thoughts on this?"*, *"How do you feel about that experience?"*, or *"Can you share more about what it means to you?"* invite deeper dialogue.
- **Approach Every Interaction with Curiosity:** Ask about someone's background, experiences, and perspective genuinely. Curiosity opens doors to empathy and insight.

According to communication experts like **Edward T. Hall**, cross-cultural misunderstandings often arise from different communication styles and norms. For instance, some cultures value indirect communication, while others prioritize directness. Being open-minded helps bridge these differences by encouraging respectful exchanges.

Recognizing and Addressing Your Own Biases

Everyone has biases—beliefs formed by our experiences, education, media, and culture. Recognizing these biases is the first step in preventing misunderstandings and building inclusive communication.

- **Self-Reflection:** Take time to reflect on your assumptions. Ask yourself, *"Am I judging someone based on stereotypes?"* or *"What experiences have shaped the way I view this person or situation?"*
- **Seek Diverse Perspectives:** Surround yourself with people from various backgrounds and actively engage with their stories and viewpoints.
- **Be Open to Feedback:** Listen to constructive feedback about how your words or actions may be perceived. Accept it with an open mind rather than defensiveness.

Studies have shown that self-awareness and empathy are crucial components of **effective intercultural communication** (Journal of Communication, 2019). Recognizing your biases and actively challenging assumptions allows for more authentic connections and reduces interpersonal conflicts.

Collaborative Communication Across Diverse Backgrounds

Working and communicating with people from different backgrounds strengthens your ability to **solve problems creatively, innovate**, and **find inclusive solutions**.

- **Team Diversity Encourages Innovation:** Diverse teams bring together multiple viewpoints, experiences, and problem-solving strategies, which often result in more creative and effective outcomes.
- **Cross-Cultural Collaboration Builds Resilience:** Facing differences and resolving conflicts within diverse teams enhances your ability to handle challenges in adaptable and inclusive ways.
- **Empathy Fuels Effective Problem-Solving:** Collaborating across cultures helps you develop empathy, which allows you to connect with others' perspectives and motivations, making teamwork more productive and cohesive.

For example, global companies like **Google and Apple** emphasize cultural diversity in their communication practices to drive innovation and success. Their commitment to cross-cultural collaboration highlights the benefits of diverse perspectives in creative problem-solving and global decision-making.

Effective communication across cultures and experiences is not just a skill—it's an ongoing practice of curiosity, respect, empathy, and adaptability. By committing to these principles, you build not only better connections but also stronger communities, workplaces, and a more inclusive world where every voice and experience matters.

Local Connections, Global Strength

Local actions can drive global change. Supporting community initiatives and collaborating with people around you not only strengthens your local area but also connects you to broader movements worldwide.

Learn from communities around the globe. Every culture and society brings unique insights and solutions. What works in a local community might inspire change in another city, country, or continent.

Support global initiatives by participating in local activities and spreading awareness about global causes. Use social media to share stories, bring attention to international issues, and encourage others to take collective action.

Your commitment to diversity, inclusion, and community builds a network of connections that transcend borders. These connections remind you that **every local challenge has a global dimension**, and every small action contributes to a collective global impact.

By embracing diversity, fostering inclusion, and committing to community growth, you lay the foundation for a world that values respect, creativity, and cooperation. This foundation builds resilience, encourages collaboration, and amplifies progress—on both a local and global scale.

7

Overcoming Challenges – Resilience in the Face of Adversity

Facing Setbacks with Grace

Setbacks are often seen as failures, but in reality, they're **opportunities wrapped in challenges**. Every setback carries a lesson, a chance to build resilience, and a moment to reflect deeply on your goals and path. In a world where change is constant and trends come and go almost overnight, setbacks require a deeper kind of engagement—one that demands reflection, strategy, and an ability to turn difficulties into meaningful progress.

As a member of Gen Z, you've grown up navigating a world filled with **rapid technological changes, social media culture, fleeting trends**, and **ephemeral attention spans**. This landscape has made you familiar with fast-paced interactions and quick updates, but setbacks push you to slow down, reassess, and engage with challenges on a much deeper level.

They invite you to take a step back, analyze the situation critically, and find constructive ways to move forward.

Rather than viewing setbacks as roadblocks that prevent progress, see them as **stepping stones that pave the path to growth, creativity**, and **understanding**.

Every obstacle contains the potential to learn something new about yourself, your strengths, and your ability to adapt and persevere. Embracing setbacks with grace means facing difficulties head-on, **acknowledging your limitations**, and using these experiences as opportunities to build **resilience and wisdom**.

Handling Criticism and Opposition

Criticism and opposition are inevitable parts of life, whether you're working on a social initiative, starting a business, or pursuing a creative passion. You will encounter people who challenge your decisions, question your commitment, and doubt your vision. And while facing criticism is uncomfortable, it is also a vital opportunity for personal and professional development.

Criticism often reveals more about **the perspectives and biases of others** than about your own work. People's viewpoints are shaped by their personal experiences, beliefs, and interests. Recognizing this helps you to see criticism not as an attack but as **a chance to gain insights and constructive feedback**.

The first step in dealing with criticism is **listening without defensiveness**. When someone challenges you, take a moment to truly hear what they're saying. Ask thoughtful questions to clarify their perspective. What are they really trying to communicate? What insights might their feedback provide that you hadn't considered? Often, criticism is a chance to improve, refine your work, and strengthen your purpose.

Moreover, it's essential to distinguish **constructive criticism from destructive feedback**. Constructive criticism aims to support your improvement, offering actionable advice that helps you grow.

Destructive criticism, on the other hand, is often rooted in personal insecurities or biases and seeks to undermine rather than uplift. Learn to recognize when someone is genuinely invested in your progress and when they are just projecting their own issues.

Respond to criticism with **respect, curiosity, and calm determination**. Thank the person for their feedback, acknowledge their perspective, and then decide whether to adjust your approach or stand firm in your purpose. Sometimes, embracing valid feedback means making necessary changes. Other times, it means reaffirming your commitment and moving forward with renewed focus and confidence.

Turning Obstacles into Opportunities for Growth

Obstacles are not barriers; they're chances to **learn, innovate**, and **transform**. Every challenge offers an opportunity to rethink strategies, develop new solutions, and ultimately, grow stronger. Some of the most significant breakthroughs and insights come from difficult situations where creative problem-solving becomes a necessity.

Think of obstacles as **tests of your creativity, adaptability**, and **resilience**. When faced with a problem, you often have to think outside the box and reevaluate your approach. This kind of problem-solving forces you to become more agile, adaptable, and resourceful. In a fast-paced world where trends change daily, adaptability is not just a survival skill—it's a competitive edge.

Consider climate activists as an example. They face **logistical challenges, financial hurdles, and social resistance**, but these obstacles have led to groundbreaking innovations, such as **sustainable technologies, eco-friendly startups**, and **powerful digital campaigns**. Such challenges don't just highlight problems; they drive the creation of solutions that benefit society on a larger scale.

Instead of automatically seeing obstacles as setbacks, **reframe your mindset** to view them as opportunities. Ask yourself thoughtful questions:

- What am I learning about myself through this experience?

- What new skills could I develop right now that will be valuable in the future?
- How can overcoming this obstacle strengthen my resolve and commitment?

This approach fosters **problem-solving skills, creativity**, and **resilience**, making you not just a survivor but an innovator. When you face challenges, prioritize **action over inaction**. Create a plan, gather your resources, and take practical steps to address the issue at hand. It's about taking proactive steps rather than falling into despair, and it transforms challenges into meaningful action and progress.

The Transformative Power of Resilience

Resilience is not just about enduring hardships; it's about **emerging stronger, wiser**, and **more capable than before**. Every setback and obstacle offers a chance to develop resilience by teaching you **persistence, adaptability**, and **self-reflection**. Resilience means bouncing back from difficulties with a clearer sense of purpose and an understanding of what you're truly capable of.

By facing setbacks head-on with a commitment to growth, you cultivate a mindset of **strength and self-assurance**. You learn that setbacks are **not the end**, but rather **critical moments of insight, creativity**, and **self-discovery**. Whether it's learning to pivot a business strategy, improving your mental health, or refining a creative project, each obstacle is a chance to grow.

As you develop resilience, you become **more adaptable to change, more open to innovation**, and more committed to your goals. You realize that setbacks are not just moments of loss or defeat; they are the **foundation of your character, the bedrock of your creativity**, and the driving force behind your ability to contribute positively to your community and the world around you.

In the end, setbacks and obstacles are opportunities to **build resilience, sharpen your problem-solving skills**, and cultivate a **stronger, clearer purpose**. Facing challenges with a commitment to action and reflection transforms obstacles into powerful stepping stones, helping you become not just a survivor of difficulties but a leader, innovator, and agent of change.

The Power of Resilience

Resilience is about more than just surviving tough situations—it's about **thriving in the face of adversity**, learning from challenges, and coming out stronger on the other side. It's a mental, emotional, and practical tool that empowers you to **adapt, grow, and ultimately succeed**, even in the most difficult circumstances.

When setbacks occur, resilient individuals don't see them as defeats but as **stepping stones that contribute to growth and progress**. They recognize that setbacks reveal strengths you never knew existed and provide lessons that foster **critical**

thinking, strategic decision-making, and **emotional balance**.

In fact, resilience cultivates a more flexible mindset, allowing you to **pivot quickly, find creative solutions**, and **maintain focus under pressure**.

Being resilient means embracing **uncertainty, ambiguity**, and **change** with open-mindedness. Instead of fearing what might go wrong, resilient people see what could go right. They don't let failure paralyze them but use it as fuel to drive forward momentum. The key is transforming obstacles from discouraging moments into **opportunities for insight, learning**, and **innovation**.

Practical Steps to Build Resilience

Start by nurturing **self-compassion**. It's easy to fall into self-criticism when things don't go as planned, but self-compassion involves treating yourself with **kindness and patience**. Speak to yourself as you would speak to a close friend. Acknowledge your setbacks without harsh judgment.

Ask yourself: *"What would I say to someone I care about in this situation?"* Practicing self-compassion helps reduce stress and builds inner strength, making it easier to tackle future challenges with a more balanced mindset.

Surround yourself with a **support system of people who uplift you**. Your network of friends, mentors, and community members plays a crucial role in resilience. These are the people who celebrate your wins, encourage you during setbacks, and offer honest but supportive advice. A strong support system provides **perspectives beyond your own, emotional stability**, and practical guidance.

Whether it's seeking advice from a mentor, chatting with a friend, or participating in group discussions, being connected to a community **reinforces accountability** and **offers encouragement**.

Additionally, **commit to lifelong learning**. Resilient people never stop growing. They're always curious and open to new experiences. Read widely, explore different disciplines, and seek knowledge that challenges your perspective and sharpens your skills.

Continuous learning builds confidence and adaptability. It allows you to gain insights from different fields, apply new techniques, and **view problems from multiple angles**. This approach not only strengthens your problem-solving abilities but also prepares you to handle unforeseen situations with more confidence and agility.

Emotional Intelligence as a Resilience Tool

Emotional intelligence (EI) is at the heart of resilience. It enables you to **understand, manage**, and **express your emotions in a constructive way**. EI also includes empathy, which allows you to **relate to others**, understand their challenges, and collaborate more effectively. When you're emotionally intelligent, you handle interpersonal conflicts better, work more efficiently in teams, and develop deeper connections.

These social interactions often serve as opportunities for **collective growth and mutual support**, strengthening your network and resilience at the same time.

Moreover, resilience means being **comfortable with discomfort**. Life doesn't come with guarantees, and uncertainty is a given. Embracing challenges with a mindset that welcomes discomfort as a teacher rather than a threat strengthens your ability to remain calm and focused even in high-pressure environments. This mental flexibility ensures that you remain **strategic, decisive**, and **purpose-driven**, regardless of setbacks.

Action Over Inertia

Resilience is built through **action**. It's about taking proactive steps rather than waiting for things to improve on their own. Each setback you face is a chance to **reflect, reassess, plan**, and **act**. Set clear, achievable goals, break them into actionable steps, and follow through with commitment. Each small action not only moves you closer to your objectives but also strengthens your capacity to tackle bigger challenges with confidence.

Look at individuals who exemplify resilience, like **entrepreneurs, activists, and artists**. They often face extreme criticism, financial challenges, or social obstacles. Yet, they use these challenges as opportunities to **innovate, pivot**, and **refine their approaches**.

Their stories highlight that resilience is about making strategic choices, adapting quickly, and remaining committed to your purpose, even when circumstances aren't ideal. Facing setbacks with grace is about more than enduring failure—it's about **transforming difficulty into resilience, criticism into insight, and obstacles into opportunities for progress**.

In the fast-paced world that Gen Z lives in, resilience and adaptability are not just about personal growth—they are the core of collective change.

You're in a position of power. Your social networks, your creativity, your access to digital tools, and your commitment to social and environmental causes mean that you have the resources to turn setbacks into progress. Every setback is an invitation to learn, a chance to innovate, and an opportunity to drive change.

Embrace setbacks as teachers. Respect criticism as a chance to improve. Use obstacles as opportunities to grow stronger.

In doing so, you don't just grow—you transform into a leader, an innovator, and an activist with purpose, ready to face challenges head-on, make meaningful change, and contribute to a world that is stronger, smarter, and more resilient.

8

Mental Health – Staying Strong for the Long Run

Recognizing Mental Health Challenges

Life today often feels like an endless balancing act.

You're expected to succeed academically, maintain social connections, excel in jobs or internships, and still carve out time for personal growth and self-care. On top of that, there are societal pressures to present a perfect image online, meet financial expectations, and prepare for an uncertain future. These demands accumulate, and before you know it, your mental health might start to take a back seat without you even realizing it.

It's not just about feeling stressed or tired; it's about experiencing a deeper, ongoing sense of disconnection, confusion, or inner struggle. You might find yourself **easily overwhelmed**,

losing interest in things you once loved, or **experiencing sudden emotional swings**.

Concentration becomes a battle, motivation dwindles, and small tasks seem disproportionately difficult. These aren't minor inconveniences—they're **signs that your mental well-being requires your attention** and care.

Why Mental Health Challenges Are So Prevalent Now

Recent studies show that young people, particularly Gen Z, are experiencing **higher levels of mental distress than any previous generation**. Research conducted by the American Psychological Association highlights that factors like **social media use, economic instability**, and **job insecurity** are significant contributors.

The constant presence of social media, for example, often means an overwhelming comparison culture where success, wealth, and happiness seem more accessible and attainable than they actually are. This can lead to feelings of **inadequacy, low self-worth**, and **heightened anxiety**.

Moreover, the current **economic landscape** adds its own layer of pressure. Gen Z faces challenges like **student debt, job market uncertainty**, and **financial instability**, which only exacerbate feelings of stress and burnout. Many young people are stepping into a world where opportunities are not as plentiful as they once were, and stability is harder to secure.

The rise of **technological integration in every part of life** also impacts mental health. While technology offers connectivity and learning opportunities, it often results in **disrupted sleep patterns, reduced face-to-face interactions**, and **information overload**. Studies have shown that excessive screen time can affect sleep quality, increase stress, and reduce overall cognitive functioning.

Recognizing Mental Health Issues Early

The first step in taking care of your mental health is recognizing that these challenges aren't just passing inconveniences— they're **important indicators that require attention**. Mental health issues like **stress, anxiety, burnout, and depression** are not temporary states that resolve on their own. Ignoring these feelings allows problems to grow, leading to more serious mental health concerns that affect **relationships, academics, career opportunities**, and **overall life satisfaction**.

It's essential to check in with yourself regularly. Ask questions like:

- *Am I feeling consistently exhausted, even after rest?*
- *Do I find it difficult to focus on things I once enjoyed?*
- *Am I experiencing mood changes that I can't easily explain?*
- *Do I feel disconnected from friends, family, or even myself?*

Recognizing these feelings early means you're taking proactive steps to address your mental health rather than waiting until it becomes unmanageable.

Building Strategies for Mental Resilience

Addressing mental health challenges early creates a foundation of resilience that supports your well-being in the long run. Here are some practical strategies to help build mental resilience:

1. **Create a Daily Routine with Boundaries**
2. Establishing a daily routine that includes clear boundaries between **work, study, social life**, and **rest** can make a significant difference. Allocate specific times to sleep, exercise, study, and downtime. When you have a structure, it becomes easier to manage responsibilities without letting stress spill over into your personal time.
3. **Engage in Physical Activity**
4. Exercise isn't just good for your body—it's a powerful mental health tool. Physical activity increases **endorphins**, which improve mood, reduce anxiety, and help you think more clearly. Whether it's a walk, a run, yoga, or a dance workout, find something that you enjoy and make it a regular habit.
5. **Practice Mindfulness and Meditation**
6. Mindfulness exercises and meditation help reduce anxiety by keeping you present. Even short, five-minute sessions can help you regain focus and calm. Apps like **Headspace** or **Calm** offer guided exercises that are accessible and practical for beginners.
7. **Talk to Someone**

8. Don't underestimate the importance of speaking with someone you trust, whether it's a friend, mentor, or mental health professional. Therapy sessions or peer discussions help you **gain perspective**, **receive support**, and **reduce the isolation** that mental struggles often bring.
9. **Limit Social Media Use**
10. Take active steps to reduce your social media time. Schedule 'no-phone' hours or use apps that limit screen time. Curate your social media experience so that it uplifts rather than drains. Follow accounts that bring value, knowledge, and positivity.

The Road to Resilience Is Not a Straight Path

Improving mental health is a continuous journey. Some days will be better than others, and setbacks are natural. The important thing is not to let challenges deter your commitment to self-care. Acknowledge setbacks, practice patience, and remind yourself that **every experience, even difficult ones, offers learning opportunities**.

Many successful individuals, especially those in **entrepreneurship, activism**, and **creative industries**, have spoken about their struggles with mental health and how those experiences shaped their resilience.

For example, **Simone Biles**, the world-renowned gymnast, openly discussed mental health struggles at a peak moment in her career, highlighting the importance of prioritizing mental well-being over professional success.

Mental health isn't just about feeling good—it's about **functioning effectively, maintaining meaningful relationships**, and **working toward your aspirations without sacrificing your well-being**.

Life today, with its challenges and pressures, offers an opportunity to cultivate mental resilience through mindful habits, social connections, and proactive care.

By prioritizing your mental health now, you're not only setting yourself up for a more stable and successful present but also laying the groundwork for a more resilient, adaptable, and meaningful future.

Remember, seeking support, setting boundaries, and committing to self-care aren't signs of weakness—**they're acts of strength and self-respect**. You're not alone, and with the right strategies, support, and mindset, you can build resilience that lasts a lifetime.

Self-Care Isn't Selfish

Self-care is not a selfish act—it's a necessary investment in yourself. When you prioritize your well-being, you're laying the groundwork for stronger relationships, clearer decision-making, and better resilience.

It equips you to handle challenges with composure and pursue your goals with clarity and determination. Here's how you can integrate self-care into your life in meaningful, sustainable ways.

Prioritize Sleep—Rest Is Your Superpower

Sleep isn't just about resting—it's about **restoring your mental health, sharpening focus**, and **replenishing your emotional resilience**. Studies show that young people often sacrifice sleep to meet deadlines or social commitments, but a lack of sleep can have long-term effects on mental health, decision-making, and overall well-being (National Sleep Foundation, 2021).

- Aim for **7-8 hours of sleep each night**.
- Establish a **consistent sleep-wake schedule**, even on weekends.
- Create a **wind-down routine** before bed: dim lights, limit screen time, and try activities like reading or light stretching.
- Practice a few minutes of **deep breathing or meditation** before sleep to calm your mind.

Prioritizing sleep allows your brain to process experiences, consolidate memories, and manage emotions effectively.

Nutrition—Fuel Your Mind and Body

What you eat has a profound impact on your mental health and energy levels. A balanced diet doesn't just support your body— it fuels your mental clarity and focus.

- Eat a variety of foods that include **lean proteins, whole grains, fruits, vegetables**, and **healthy fats**.
- Limit processed foods and excessive sugar, as they can contribute to **mood swings and mental fog**.
- Stay hydrated. Even mild dehydration can affect **concentration, energy levels**, and **decision-making**.

Nutrition acts as the building block for your mental resilience. A well-nourished body supports a sharper mind and a more balanced emotional state.

Regular Exercise—Strengthen Your Body, Empower Your Mind

Exercise is a powerful mental health tool. Physical activity releases **endorphins**, which reduce stress and boost your mood (Mayo Clinic, 2020). It's not about looking good but about feeling good and staying resilient.

- It doesn't have to be a full workout. A **short walk, a quick stretching session**, or even a few push-ups can help.
- Incorporating regular movement into your day improves

focus, boosts energy levels, and enhances **mental clarity**.
- Activities like **yoga or running** serve as excellent outlets for stress, helping you clear your mind and build resilience.

Even brief physical activity can provide a mental reset, transforming stress into focus and resilience into clarity.

Mindfulness and Reflection—Ground Your Thoughts

Mindfulness practices aren't just trendy—they're tools for **stability, self-awareness**, and **emotional balance**. Techniques like meditation and journaling help you observe your thoughts, reduce overwhelm, and find clarity.

- **Meditation:** Start with just five minutes a day. Focus on your breath and let thoughts come and go without judgment.
- **Journaling:** Write about your experiences, your emotions, and your goals. Ask yourself:
- *What am I grateful for today?*
- *What challenges am I facing, and how can I approach them differently?*
- *How am I feeling, and what can I do to take care of myself right now?*

These practices cultivate inner resilience, teaching you how to handle emotions without letting them dictate your life.

Setting Boundaries—Learn When to Say "No"

Boundaries are not about rejection; they're about **respecting your time, energy**, and **emotional space**. Setting limits helps you protect your well-being, ensuring that you have more energy and commitment to what truly matters.

- **Evaluate Social Commitments:** Attend events and gatherings that uplift and energize you rather than drain your energy.
- **Career and Academic Boundaries:** Don't overcommit. Focus on delivering quality work rather than trying to please everyone.
- **Personal Time:** Treat personal time as sacred. Use it to recharge, reflect, and invest in things that bring **joy and purpose**.

Saying "no" is about maintaining **balance and focus**. It allows you to invest your energy where it counts, ensuring sustainability in your efforts and long-term resilience.

Build a Support System—Strength in Connection

Self-care isn't a solo journey. It's about **leaning on people who lift you up, provide constructive feedback**, and offer emotional support. A strong support system can provide encouragement, guidance, and a safety net during tough times.

- Surround yourself with people who encourage your growth and bring positivity into your life.
- Talk to mentors, friends, or professionals who offer advice without judgment.
- Engage with **communities that share your interests**, whether it's academic, creative, or social. Communities strengthen resilience by offering shared knowledge, support, and encouragement.

Studies show that having a support system not only boosts mental health but also increases your ability to tackle challenges with a sense of collective wisdom and resilience (American Psychological Association, 2019).

Self-care is about investing in yourself so that you can invest in everything else that matters to you—your goals, your relationships, your education, and your community. It's about being strong enough to handle challenges, focused enough to make progress, and resilient enough to bounce back from setbacks.

Simple, sustainable self-care routines—like prioritizing sleep, eating well, staying active, practicing mindfulness, setting boundaries, and building a support system—don't just support your mental health. They build resilience, clarity, and a foundation for long-term success.

Remember: **Self-care isn't just for you**—it's your commitment to everything you care about, ensuring that you can show up fully, authentically, and resiliently in every area of your life.

Creating Support Networks

No one thrives alone.

Having a support system—friends, mentors, professionals—makes a huge difference in mental health. Surround yourself with people who uplift, listen, and offer constructive support.

Talk to someone you trust about what you're experiencing. This could be a close friend, a family member, or a mental health professional.

Talking helps clarify your feelings and often brings relief. Additionally, many schools, universities, and workplaces have mental health resources, like counselors or peer support groups. Don't hesitate to seek these out.

Build **peer networks or support circles** where mental health is openly discussed. These groups aren't just about socializing; they're about sharing strategies, encouraging each other, and standing together through challenges.

Being part of a community that prioritizes mental well-being helps normalize self-care and resilience.

Remember, seeking support is a strength, not a weakness. It allows you to face challenges with clarity and determination rather than isolation and overwhelm.

The Long-Term Power of Resilience

Resilience isn't a momentary act—it's a lifelong mindset. It's about bouncing back but also *bouncing forward*, learning from experiences, and coming out stronger.

Resilient individuals don't just survive; they adapt and thrive. They turn failures into lessons and mistakes into stepping stones. For example, many successful people started with setbacks but used those experiences to build resilience.

Build resilience by embracing **failure as part of the journey**. Each setback is a chance to learn something new about yourself and your abilities. Reflect on what didn't work, why it didn't work, and how you can approach it differently next time.

Practice gratitude as a mental habit. Take a few minutes every day to write down or think about three things you're grateful for. Gratitude shifts your focus from what's missing to what you have, strengthening mental clarity and balance.

Resilience grows with **small victories**, consistent routines, and a mindset that prioritizes long-term progress over short-term convenience. It's not about perfection; it's about persistence, learning, and growing, step by step.

9

The Future – What's Next for Gen Z Change-Makers?

A Vision for the Future

The future isn't a passive event—it's a canvas on which **your choices, actions, and vision** will be painted. As a member of Gen Z, you're not just inheriting the world—you're actively shaping it. You have the tools, the creativity, and the commitment to drive sustainable progress across **environmental sustainability, technology, education**, and the workplace.

The actions you take today will create a foundation for a more equitable, sustainable, and inclusive world tomorrow.

Environmental Sustainability: Small Actions, Big Impact

Environmental sustainability is no longer a distant goal—it's a responsibility and a reality that calls for **immediate, actionable steps**.

- **Support Clean Energy Initiatives:** Support renewable energy projects and invest time in learning about sustainable energy solutions. Participate in initiatives like **solar installations, community wind projects**, and **clean transportation systems**.
- **Reduce Waste and Embrace Circular Economy Practices:** Whether it's **composting, upcycling**, or **participating in swap events**, you're contributing to a system where waste is minimized and resources are reused efficiently.
- **Promote Sustainable Agriculture:** Support local farms that use eco-friendly methods, or get involved in community gardens. Understand where your food comes from and push for **agriculture that prioritizes soil health and biodiversity**.

Practical Habit Changes:

- Start **refusing single-use plastics**, prioritizing reusable bags, and supporting **eco-friendly brands** that practice transparency and sustainability in their supply chain (sources like **Sustainable Brands and Green Business Journal** show companies prioritizing these practices).
- Use platforms like **Good On You**, which rates brands based on their environmental and ethical practices, helping consumers make informed choices.

Ethical Innovation in Technology: Redefining Digital Progress

As **digital natives**, you are in a prime position to shape technology in a way that prioritizes **transparency, ethics**, and **social responsibility**.

- **Advocate for Data Privacy and Transparency:** Demand accountability from companies about how your data is used. Support initiatives that call for **clear data privacy policies** and transparency in **AI algorithms** and digital tools.
- **Push for Inclusive Algorithms:** Technology should reflect **diversity, equity**, and **inclusion**. This means advocating for systems that don't discriminate based on race, gender, or socioeconomic background. Initiatives like **Algorithmic Justice League** highlight the push for more ethical AI practices.
- **Promote Tech that Educates and Connects:** Focus on creating platforms and tools that foster **collaborative learning, digital literacy**, and **positive social interactions**. Technology should be a means to share knowledge, connect communities, and promote creativity, rather than isolate or exploit.
-

Education Reform: Preparing for Life, Not Just Tests

Education should go beyond **standardized tests** and focus on preparing individuals for real-world experiences and challenges.

- **Advocate for Personalized Learning Systems:** Schools and learning platforms should embrace methods that **cater to different learning speeds, strengths**, and **interests**, fostering true engagement and understanding.
- **Incorporate Practical Life Skills:** Integrate **financial literacy, critical thinking, emotional intelligence**, and **real-world problem-solving** into school curriculums. Practical education systems should equip students to **make informed decisions, manage finances**, and **navigate life's challenges confidently**.
- **Equal Access to Quality Education:** Campaign for reforms that address **education inequity, teacher support**, and **community resources**, ensuring every student, regardless of background, has the tools to succeed. Research shows that **community-based educational initiatives often close achievement gaps** (National Educational Policy Center).

The Future Workplace: A Commitment to Purpose and Sustainability

The workplace is where purpose-driven change meets practicality. It should be a place of **respect, purpose**, and **long-term commitment to sustainability and social impact**.

- **Push for Ethical Work Cultures:** Demand workplaces that prioritize **fair wages, respectful labor practices**, and **em-**

ployee well-being. Companies like **Patagonia and Interface** demonstrate sustainable labor practices and corporate responsibility.

- **Promote Environmental Responsibility in Business Practices:** Support companies that commit to **carbon neutrality, eco-friendly operations**, and **sustainable sourcing**.
- **Purpose-Driven Goals Over Profit Margins:** Advocate for companies to align with **social impact initiatives, diversity efforts**, and **community support projects** rather than just profit-driven metrics.

Practical Steps to Implement Change:

- Propose **sustainable office policies, eco-friendly commuting options**, and **regular workshops on mental health, career development**, and **environmental responsibility**.
- Support platforms like **Ethical Consumer and Fairtrade organizations**, which evaluate companies based on their social and environmental responsibility.

Sustained Change Through Practical Action

Long-term change isn't about grand gestures—it's about **small, consistent actions that build momentum**.

- Join **local environmental groups, participate in clean-up drives,** and support initiatives that prioritize community well-being.
- Start or join initiatives on **social media platforms that raise awareness, educate followers about sustainability**, and

encourage community engagement.

- Collaborate with peers to **develop apps and platforms that support mental health, education access**, and **community collaboration**, showing how technology can be a force for good.

Research from organizations like the UNDP and the Sustainable Development Goals (SDGs) highlights that **small community-driven initiatives** often lead to long-lasting change that affects entire cities and countries, driving progress on **sustainability, equality**, and **social development**.

Guiding Gen Alpha – Mentorship and Responsibility

As a member of Gen Z, your role extends beyond self-discovery—you're shaping the path for **Gen Alpha**, a generation growing up in a world that is more **digitally connected, socially aware**, and **environmentally conscious** than ever before. Your experiences, decisions, and guidance will lay the foundation for how they **learn, grow**, and **impact the world**.

Mentorship here isn't just about advice; it's about setting examples, instilling resilience, and fostering habits that prioritize **critical thinking, creativity**, and **mental health**.

Mentorship as Shared Experience

Mentorship is not about presenting a flawless image—it's about sharing **your real experiences**, including your mistakes and challenges. Gen Alpha thrives on seeing mentors who demonstrate that:

- **Failure is a Stepping Stone:** Show them that failure is not a setback but a chance to learn and improve. Studies have shown that experiencing setbacks in formative years often builds **resilience and adaptability** (source: *Psychological Science Journal*).
- **Growth Comes from Challenges:** Emphasize that persistence and collaboration are not ideals but **practical, actionable tools for success**. Whether it's in school, sports, or creative projects, teamwork teaches cooperation and mutual respect.

Share your own stories of struggle and triumph. These authentic moments make mentorship relatable and show that resilience is a skill developed through experience, not just an abstract concept.

Fostering Critical Thinking and Creativity

Encourage Gen Alpha to **question norms, explore alternatives**, and **think critically**. This is where mentorship becomes about nurturing curiosity instead of promoting conformity.

- **Ask Open-Ended Questions:** Instead of giving solutions, ask, *"What do you think we could do differently here?"* or *"Why do you think that choice might work?"* These questions stimulate **problem-solving skills** and **independent thought**.
- **Encourage Exploration Across Disciplines:** Introduce them to fields beyond their immediate interests. For instance, combining **science with art or math with music** can spark creativity and innovation. Research indicates that interdisciplinary learning boosts creativity and cognitive flexibility (source: *Educational Psychology Review*).
- **Support Experimentation Over Perfection:** Whether they're coding a project, painting a picture, or writing a story, encourage them to focus on **process over product**, helping them learn through experimentation rather than perfection.

Prioritizing Emotional Intelligence and Mental Health

Emotional mentorship is about teaching the importance of **self-care, resilience**, and **mental well-being**—not as weaknesses but as strengths that form the backbone of sustainable progress.

- **Normalize Asking for Help:** Show that seeking support is a strength, not a vulnerability. Whether it's from peers, mentors, or professionals, prioritizing mental health is a sign of **self-awareness** and **emotional intelligence**.
- **Introduce Mindfulness Practices:** Activities like **journaling, meditation,** or **daily reflection** can help Gen Alpha manage stress and maintain focus. Studies have shown that mindfulness practices can improve **concentration,**

reduce anxiety, and **enhance overall mental health** (source: *Mindfulness Studies Journal*).

- **Be a Role Model of Balance:** Prioritize your own mental health by maintaining **boundaries, practicing self-care**, and being transparent about struggles. This visibility helps normalize self-care as an essential habit rather than an afterthought.

Instilling Responsibility and Social Awareness

Mentorship means guiding younger generations to **act with purpose, responsibility**, and **social consciousness**.

- **Community Engagement Initiatives:** Encourage participation in **clean-up drives, social projects**, and **local volunteering efforts**. Such activities teach the value of **community responsibility** and **social impact**.
- **Environmental Awareness from a Young Age:** Show practical ways they can support sustainability, like **reducing waste, saving water**, and **supporting eco-friendly brands**.
- **Advocacy and Activism:** Support their involvement in movements that promote **social justice, environmental sustainability**, and **equal education opportunities**. Studies highlight that young activists often bring fresh perspectives and determination to social movements (source: *Youth Activism Studies Journal*).

Building a Legacy of Purpose and Resilience

By mentoring Gen Alpha, you're planting seeds of **resilience, creativity**, and **social responsibility** that will grow into sustained progress and innovation.

- **Encourage Continuous Learning and Curiosity:** Teach them that **education is a lifelong journey**, where every challenge is an opportunity, and every success, a reason to explore more deeply.
- **Cultivate a Purpose-Driven Approach:** Whether they seek careers in **technology, arts, education**, or **business**, instill a commitment to **ethical leadership, environmental responsibility**, and **social purpose**.

The mentorship you offer becomes a **legacy** that transcends generations, ensuring that each successive group of change-makers remains committed to **innovation, sustainability**, and **social responsibility**.

By fostering resilience, creativity, and responsibility early on, you equip Gen Alpha with the tools to create a world that is not just successful but also **compassionate, resilient, and **purpose-driven**. The responsibility you take on as a mentor is not just about personal impact—it's about ensuring that progress is sustained by generations committed to collective growth, creativity, and respect for people and the planet alike.

Expanding Your Influence – From Local to Global

Your influence begins at the local level but holds the potential to drive **widespread, systemic change**. Whether in politics, business, or community initiatives, your ideas, actions, and voice are powerful tools for shaping a better future.

In politics, your engagement is a force for progress. Voting is just one piece of the puzzle—get involved in community meetings, propose initiatives, or join local boards. Local policies often have a domino effect, shaping broader regional, national, and even global outcomes. Your participation sends a message to decision-makers and shows that young voices are not only present but **purpose-driven and committed**.

In business, the landscape is shifting. More companies today recognize that **sustainability and social responsibility** are not optional—they're necessary. You, as a new leader, can drive businesses to prioritize **ethics, transparency**, and **community impact**. Support brands that align with your values, and consider starting your own venture where profit serves a purpose rather than the other way around.

Purpose-driven businesses can drive change that prioritizes **people, the environment**, and **long-term social impact**.

In the corporate world, aim to build environments where diversity isn't just a box to check—it's a source of innovation and strength. Advocate for inclusive cultures where employees feel respected, creativity flourishes, and collaboration brings about meaningful progress.

Companies thrive when their teams are **diverse, motivated**, and **well-supported**, contributing positively not only within the organization but also to the community and environment.

Ultimately, your commitment to these areas transforms **cultures, reshapes attitudes**, and turns business and leadership into powerful forces for **good, sustainability**, and **collective responsibility**.

Change isn't just about profits or policies; it's about creating systems that prioritize **well-being, responsibility**, and **lasting progress**, setting the stage for a future where success is measured by social impact, ethical responsibility, and global resilience.

Leaving a Lasting Legacy

Every change-maker leaves a legacy. This isn't about fame or personal success—it's about impact, continuity, and inspiration. The mark you leave is in the communities you strengthen, the systems you reform, and the people you uplift.

Reflect on what you want to be remembered for. Are you committed to **social equity, environmental responsibility, or technological advancement**? Your legacy could be in mentoring others, advocating for policy changes, or building initiatives that support your community long-term.

Inspire others by being authentic. Share your journey—the good, the bad, and the ugly. Talk about your failures and what those moments taught you. Transparency builds trust and encourages others to take risks, make mistakes, and learn from them.

Pass the torch by actively supporting new leaders, sharing resources, and promoting initiatives that align with your vision. Whether it's through mentorship, funding community projects, or collaborating with others, your commitment to continuity ensures that the changes you started will carry forward.

Your legacy isn't just about sustaining progress—it's about igniting future movements, creating solutions that stand the test of time, and leaving a world that is more inclusive, sustainable, and just than the one you inherited.

By focusing on purpose, resilience, and continuity, you don't just change your world—you build a future where everyone thrives, communities prosper, and change becomes an ongoing, unstoppable force.

Conclusion: We Are the Change

As a member of Gen Z, you stand at the forefront of a movement—a movement that's bigger than trends, bigger than social media clout, and bigger than personal ambition. It's a movement for sustainability, progress, social equity, and purpose-driven living. It's about shaping a world where progress is not just about speed but about **meaning,**

responsibility, and balance. You have the power to transform not only your future but the future of everyone who comes after.

Look back at everything you've learned: You're a generation of **resilience, creativity, and connectivity**. Digital tools give you unprecedented power to organize, share, and collaborate. Social awareness gives you clarity about what needs changing. And your deep-rooted commitment to progress positions you to drive change in a way that no generation before could. You're not just participants in this world—you're its architects, dreamers, and doers.

It's crucial to recognize that **change isn't a destination—it's a continuous process**. Every step you take—no matter how small—adds to a larger impact. Whether you're initiating local projects, influencing workplace cultures, or driving digital campaigns, every action shapes a system, builds a community, and lays the foundation for the next milestone of progress.

Start today. Act now.

Use your voice on social media, support businesses that share your values, innovate with purpose, and stand up for what you believe in.

Talk to your peers, mentor younger generations, and collabo-rate with people from different backgrounds and perspectives. Every interaction is a chance to learn, grow, and build.

Don't wait for change to come to you. Be the change. Be the one who asks questions, challenges norms, and never stops striving.

Stay **active, stay focused, and stay resilient**.

Every setback is a chance to adapt.

Every failure is an opportunity to learn. Every success is a stepping stone to greater action.

You are the change-makers, the leaders, the thinkers, and the creators. Your energy, creativity, and passion are forces that can heal communities, repair the environment, and reshape entire industries.

The responsibility is yours—but so is the opportunity. Embrace it fully.

Together, let's create a world that's not only sustainable but just, equitable, and empowering for all. Stand tall, stay passionate, and never stop striving. Because with you, change is unstoppable—and the future isn't just something to inherit— it's something to build, shape, and live for.

www.ingramcontent.com/pod-product-compliance
Lightning Source LLC
Chambersburg PA
CBHW061641250726
48659CB00004B/1322